Meditations With the Navajo

Prayer-Songs & Stories
of Healing and Harmony

by

Gerald Hausman

BEAR & COMPANY
SANTA FE, NEW MEXICO

Jerry Goethe

Library of Congress Cataloging-in-Publication Data
Hausman, Gerald.
  Meditations with the Navajo.
  1.Navajo Indians—Religion and mythology.
2. Navajo Indians—Philosophy. I. Title.
E99.N3H38   1987   299!78   87-19450
ISBN 0-939680-39-4

Bear & Company
P.O. Drawer 2860
Santa Fe, NM 87504

Selections from this book are available on the audio cassette, "Navajo
Nights," produced by the author, at $9.95 per copy, c/o November Moon,
Box 8377, Santa Fe, NM 87504-8377.

Design: Kathleen Katz
Illustration: Sid Hausman
Typography: Casa Sin Nombre, Ltd.
Printed in the United States of America by BookCrafters

CONTENTS

Introductions

I am continually amazed at Gerry's ability to grasp the insights and interpretations of the intricate meanings behind the stories told by the Navajo. In his new book, *Meditations with the Navajo*, he again brings forth deep mental reflections on the Navajo's psychological perceptions of their nature and wisdom.

I must point out that, in some cases, a legendary or mythological version of a story may differ among various Navajo storytellers. However, they are all fundamentally the same, with the same concluding moral or lesson. I have sat with different storytellers, in particular, Navajo medicine men who would exchange versions of the same story. One would state how he was told the story, and upon the oral conclusion of his version, he would ask the other person how he heard the same story. In this way, they would exchange story versions, which in itself is an educational process for the entire audience. It is interesting to bear witness to such a dialogue because there are no disputes or disagreements about the story's versions between the two storytellers. Each storyteller is respected for his knowledge and perceptions; whereas, among the non-Indians, there is always a precision to detail, accurateness, and competitiveness attributed to their literary works.

I have known Gerry for approximately 25 years, since our early days in college, and I have seen him mature steadily into a prolific writer on Indian literature. I feel he has once again caught the spirit of his quest in this new book.

Ray Brown
a Navajo friend of the author

 4

Gerald Hausman's *Meditations with the Navajo* is a collection of tales, poems and meditations capturing the essence of the Navajo people's way of life. There is the story of Changing Woman, the god-like ancestress who teaches the people how to live. Changing Woman finds her counterpart in the White Buffalo Calf Woman of the Sioux Nation, bringer of the Sacred Pipe and instructress of how to do things right, symbols of the power of women in Native American mythology.

There are stories of the Holy People, of First Man and First Woman; of Old Man Coyote, the artful trickster; of healings done by hand tremblers and stargazers, of creation and destruction, birth-giving and death. Witchcraft also.

Some of the tales are influenced by legends of non-Navajo tribes, particularly the Pueblos. One story about throwing eyeballs around has its origin in a Cheyenne tale in which Veeho, the schemer, is tricked into hurling his eyeballs into a tree. Another tale, about the Paiute prophet Wowoka and the Ghost Dance, is the fruit of the author's imagination.

Meditations with the Navjao is a work refreshingly unlike many others dealing with Diné mythology. It is free of the anthropologist's specialized verbiage. It speaks to people, not to the professional ethnologist. It's structure is unique. Tales in the form of poems are followed by meditations which explain and instruct. Many stories are alive with the author's personal involvement.

Navajo myths are among the most poetic in the world, full of dazzling word imagery. Hausman's meditations are likewise sheer poetry "traveling on sunbeams," about men who "cup stars in their palms, having their bare feet tickled by snakes' tongues."

The tales are, at the same time, traditional and untraditional—Navajo myths seen through the author's eyes, or rather felt by his heart—to which he gives an intensely personal, going-beneath-the-surface interpretation which provokes and beguiles.

Richard Erdoes
author of *Lame Deer, Seeker of Visions; The Sound of Flutes; The Raindance People;* and co-author of *Amercian Indian Myths and Legends.*

Author's Note:

When I first began this book in 1974 I had help—a lot of it—from a number of talented women, but especially my mother whose first sacred prayer rug, now more than fifty years old, is never far from my sight. Her heritage, her love of native ways, was always in her eyes and skin and hands. These she passed on to me, and these now belong to my two daughters, Mariah, the Wind, and Hannah, the Earth. The other important female presence in this book is Alice Winston, another writer-member of our family, who still walks on tip-toes, barefoot, while singing her morning songs. She is responsible for researching some of the meditations in this book. Thanks to Alice, to Joogii, to Ray Brown, his wife Ethel, their son Gerald, and Gerry and Barbara Clow.

Portions of this book originally appeared in *Sitting on the Blue-Eyed Bear* (Lawrence Hill & Co., 1975/Sunstone Press, 1980); *No Witness*, Stackpole, 1980; *Anasazi Honey*, Longhouse, 1980.

CHANGING WOMAN

In beauty it is done
in harmony it is written
In beauty and harmony it shall so be finished.
Changing woman said it so.

Changing Woman was born of Horizontal Woman and Upper Darkness. Found on a mountain top, she was taken home by a stranger. In twelve days, she was a big girl. In eighteen days, a complete woman. This is what she said.

"I am called Peach Blossom. On this night, all in the hogan stay awake until the dawn when the singers of songs sing the Dawn Songs of Changing Woman. Now the curtain of the hogan is torn aside and I run out toward the south for half a mile. Six young men follow me and pretend to race; I know I will beat them and this will bring much good luck. When I return, the ashes are blown off the corncake and a woman cuts a circle out of the center and divides it into parts. I take one and present it to Boy-Who-Looks-Down. He avoids my eyes, but he accepts the corncake and takes a small nibble of it. Now the sun is risen. I am a Woman."

Changing Woman Said It So

Changing Woman is not changing her hair
    to suit the times. She wears it long
    when it rains. Her black hair rains down.

Changing Woman wears her heart where
    her People can see it. She has bled
    for centuries of love, none of it wasted,
    none of it lost. Out of her heart's blood,
    the corn grows green.

Changing Woman is White Shell Woman.
    She lives in the Pacific
    where Sun Father shines.
    She gives us her blessing,
    these little shells
    we wear on our neck.

Changing Woman wears white when it is cold.
    In winter we walk softly
    upon her snowy skirt. Those who leave
    hard tracks upon her do not
    receive her blessing. Those who take
    from her, rape her—spoil her
    goodness. Those who steal
    her treasure out of the soil
    cannot know the beauty of

Changing Woman; nor can they harm her.
    For her loyalty
    is beyond our measure.

Changing Woman does not hear
    your curse—you who swear upon
    her name, you who take your own
    woman's name in vain, you who
    do not love the life she has given.
    It is a sin to swear at that which
    made you: you curse yourself.

Changing Woman was always there—
    when the ripe fruit was stolen
    from the bough, when Anai, the Enemy,
    cut the root of the peach and burned the corn
    and left hard black tracks upon her.

Still, she sweetened our bitter dreams.
    And we were suckled back from famine.
    She taught us well. She never hurt us.
    The Sun Father tried to take
    away the Twins, his sons, our first protectors.
    He let monsters roam the Earth.

If you stare at him too long,
    you go blind from his power.
    Changing Woman said it so.

The hogan is hers
    and children are hers.
    And Woman
    is rightful-owner of these
    because Changing Woman said it so.

From the clan of the mother
    comes the owner. Son of mother.
    Son, married, stays

in the clan of mother;
son's son looks to mother:
Changing Woman said it so.

From the beginning it was cast—
        the clan, the given
        name, the heart's claim: motherhood.
        Changing Woman—who changes
        four times a year.

Winter-summer-fall-spring,
        the four directions
        the four cardinal points
        the four births from the underworld
        the four breaths of life—
        Changing Woman said it so.

In beauty it is done,
in harmony it is written.
In beauty and harmony it shall so be finished.
Changing Woman said it so.

MEDITATION ON
CHANGING WOMAN

Navajos do not have a single ruling deity (just as in their society there is no ruling person or class), but rather many deities, or Holy People. These Holy People are powerful and mysterious, capricious, and capable of every human emotion. They travel on sunbeams, rainbows, lightning. They punish humans, or Earth Surface People, as willingly as they help them. A mistake in ritual can bring about disaster; the Holy People must then be coerced to give aid.

Principal among the Holy People are First Man and First Woman, Coyote, Changing Woman, and the Sun. Changing Woman is the most highly revered and the most dependable. She never harms Earth Surface People and can always be depended upon for aid. From her symbolic image comes the strength of Navajo women.

For Navajos, the natural world is divided into genders. There are male rains—heavy violent thunderstorms—and there are female rains—soft gentle showers. Earth and sheep are identified with the suffix "-mah," which means mother. Changing Woman confers female qualities upon the world, while the Sun bestows the male qualities.

Changing Woman (often referred to with the suffix "-mah") is also called Earth Woman and White Shell Woman. She is the source of life, the giver of sustenance and destiny to all beings. As the Earth goes through seasonal changes—from the growth of spring and summer to the dying of fall and the coming of winter— so Changing Woman can attain old age, die, and be reborn. She is the symbol of the Female Rains and the psyche of lakes, rivers, and mountains.

In the beginning, Changing Woman was found as a baby by First Man; she was reared by First Man and First Woman. She matured quickly, and at the time of her first menstruation a puberty rite was held to which all creatures came. Each creature offered groups of songs to bring Earth Surface People into being and to help Changing Woman to create this new race and give them the power of regeneration. This is the rite that is still held for Navajo girls entering puberty. Molded into the most beautiful of maidens and dressed in white shell, Changing Woman was given to the Sun. Navajo girls, in their puberty rites, are symbolically turned into Changing Woman, and are therefore wellsprings of beauty and abundance.

Concerning Changing Woman, the Sun made the following decree: "She will attend to her children and provide their food. Everywhere I go over the Earth, she will have charge of female rain. I myself will control the male rain. She will be in control of vegetation everywhere for the benefit of Earth People."

The symbol of the mother as the giver of life is most important. Out of the womb of Earth, Holy People emerged; from the womb of Changing Woman, ancestors of the Navajos came; from the womb of Navajo woman, the entire Navajo race comes. All relationships are traced through the womb of mother. Father brings about conception, but it is through mother that he is related to his children. Brothers and sisters are related to each other through their having been borne in the same womb. Parentage, though, places strong emphasis on the mother rather than the father.

Sun represents fatherhood and masculinity. His aspects are distance power, leadership, and discipline. Just as Earth, which Changing Woman symbolizes, is nurturing to all beings, Sun is, symbolically, a non-intimate energy source. The universe is in order when Sun and Changing Woman (Sun and Earth/man and woman/father and mother) are united.

Thus, Navajos believe that day (union of Earth and Sun) signifies good, safety, life, and growth. Night represents separation of Sun and Earth, and therefore it implies/signifies danger and potential evil.

This reverence of the nurturing female has had a great effect on the structures of Navajo life. The unity of the family is of ultimate importance for, surrounded by the belligerence of the white world, mother, father, brother and sister are mainstays of inner harmony. Yet it is always the mother who is the family's heartbeat.

Traditional Navajo families live in isolated areas. Because of the small amount of water, sparse vegetation, and scarcity of firewood, only a limited number of people can live near each other. Isolation makes the family that much tighter; and the hogan, their home, further anneals the communal bond.

Like the Earth and the womb, the hogan is round. It has a domed roof with a smoke-hole in the center and one entranceway, with a door facing east to catch the rising sun. Made of logs or railroad ties chinked with mud, hogans have been the home of the Navajo for centuries. At night, everyone sleeps together on the floor.

Although often built by the man, the hogan, like the land surrounding it, is the property of the woman. A larger family may have more than one hogan. Everyone who lives on this land will *belong* to the group because of his/her relationship to the oldest female. In one living area, the mother and father, their unmarried sons and daughters, and their married daughters with their husbands may all be together. Married sons, however, will leave home to live with the families of their wives.

Work is shared by all members of this extended family: the seeking of food, gathering of firewood, farming, caring for children, and herding sheep. Each person within the family, small children included, owns his own sheep, but the herd is kept in a central flock, which further reinforces the sense of communal life and purpose.

ANIMALS

White Hawk went out
and Sparrow Hawk followed
and White Hawk reported, "all is well."

Emergence

Before the wagon-rutted trail going north, before the deer-skin legging with its row of silver buttons on the side, before the turquoise stone set in heavy silver on a man's waist, before boiled mutton and corncakes and Mexican pesos pounded into rings and bracelets.

Before a child was lost among the owl people and led home along the cactus trail in broad daylight, with his night-shaped eyes blinking in the sun, before the hump-backed bear with blue eyes was ever sat upon, before Night Chant, Mountain Chant, Happiness Chant, Feather Chant, Bead Chant, Evil-Spirit Chant, Coyote Chant—before any Chant under the sun, before that, before that, and before that . . .

There was a hole or pit that went down into the underworld and the animals and gods came out of it. But after the fourth day of their emergence, a beautiful daughter of one of the animal chiefs was lost, and two searchers looked long and hard until they looked down into the hole that led to the underworld, and there they spied the beautiful daughter, sitting beside a stream and combing her hair: four days after, those two searchers died.

And that is why the Dead must not be touched, or even looked upon, but wrapped in a blanket and placed in an unmarked grave; the hogan burned, and the last footprints of family brushed away and smoothed, so that the departed spirit cannot find his way back after he has gone into the hole or pit, where the gods and animals were born into this world.

The Flood

Now there was no sun, moon, or stars
but in the East, White Dawn,
four-fingers high, appeared every morning.
At midday, Blue Dawn lit up the South
and in late afternoon Yellow Dawn
streaked the West.

Coyote was sent to discover
the source of the dawn,
but instead, he stole two Water Monster Babies
who lived with their parents
in two large springs.

Now the four-finger-high White Dawn
was only three fingers high
with a dark streak beneath.

Wolf Man was sent to learn what was wrong.
He returned at nightfall
and said *all was well,*
but next morning White Dawn was very narrow
and the dark below was bigger still.

So then Mountain Lion went out
and returned, saying: *all is well,*
but on the third morning
the belt of darkness
was wider than White Dawn.

So then White Hawk went out
and Sparrow Hawk followed

and White Hawk reported,
all is well,
but Sparrow Hawk said:
the water at the head of the two springs
is rising so fast
that there surely will be a terrible flood.

This was the fourth morning
and White Dawn
was wiped out
by the belt of darkness.

Now the waters rose
and all were frightened,
so the animal people gathered corn and seeds
and climbed to the top
of White Mountain in the east,
until it was swallowed up by water:
then they climbed Blue Mountain
in the south, Yellow Mountain
in the west, and Black Mountain
in the north—
and each time they climbed
one of these mountains,
they scooped up handfuls of earth
from the top
and they took one reed
from the bottom.

Now the waters rose over all
the mountains, except Black Mountain,
and here the animal people
planted a female reed in the west

and a male reed in the east,
and the waters rose higher and higher.

Then the animal people
climbed into the two reeds:
Turkey was the last
to get into his reed—
the foamy waters whitened
the tips of his tailfeathers
(they are white to this day)
and the reeds sprang up into the sky.

Now at the end of the fourth day,
the two reeds met at the top of the sky
and could go no farther,
except that Locust,
with his bow of darkness
and sacred arrows,
shot a hole in the sky
which passed on into the world above—
the world of light and dark,
First Man and First Woman,
bitter water, deer spring,
and fallen leaves.

Animals

First Man ordered Gopher underground
because he brought
toothache into the world.

Then he sent the Winged Ones
into the skies and mountains
to make their homes.

He told the Lizards
to make their homes
in the cliffs and rocks.

The Beavers and Otters
were sent to the rivers and waters.

Then he called Wolf and he said:
"You have stolen. That is wrong.
Therefore you are the Big Wanderer—
you shall travel far and wide
over the face of the Earth."

He called Snake and told him
that he was going to be given
a bag of medicine,
but since there was no place to tie it,
he would put it in his mouth.

Then First Man called
the one who stole two Water Monster Babies
and he told him his name was Coyote.
But Coyote grew furious

over this name
and said: "Such a name!"
And he declared
that he would not have it
and that he would leave,
so First Man calmed him down
and gave him another name
which was First Angry.

After that, Coyote felt better;
he had been given a great name,
or so he thought,
and he went away happy
because he was told
that whatever happened
on the face of the Earth,
he would be the first to know.

MEDITATION ON
EMERGENCE Part I

The First World is darkness, inhabited by nine people, six kinds of ants, three kinds of beetles. All people speak the same language. There are no stones, no vegetation, no light. It is a primary and simple world, containing the rudiments of action, the desire for movement. As creatures begin to explore and climb, mythical characteristics are given to them and a personal dimension is added to their existence. There is no differentiation between insects, animals, and humans. In most of the origin stories, after the initial emergence, are First Man, First Woman, First Girl, First Boy, Coyote, and Fire Deity. There is no primary creator, or God, making the world and life. Rather, creation comes about from the first stirrings of movement in the bottommost world, the first active step toward change, and continues until emergence into the Fifth World. Creation, in the Navajo sense, is conscious activity from *within*, not the external act of a greater being, as in the Old Testament story of creation, in which "God created the heavens and the Earth."

As the People move upward, First Man makes day and night. He becomes a being of power and has in his possession sacred stones and shells—Whiteshell, Turquoise, Abalone, Jet, and Red-White Stone. The concept of evil comes early, but rather than a negative phenomenon, it is a force which must be controlled and used when needed. First Man says, "I am filled with evil, yet there is a time to use it and a time to withhold it." Thus, First Man and the emerging People are not good or bad; they hold within themselves the powers of darkness and light. Neither perfection nor the elimination of evil are goals to be sought; the key is always *balance*.

Coyote plays the same part in Navajo stories as he does in other Native American tales. Trickster and troublemaker, he is an awkward buffoon, but at the same time, full of life, insight, hard-won wisdom. The freedom of his buffoonery enables him to act and speak in ways that the more conventional beings cannot. He plays Greek chorus, court jester, pointed, painful human conscience. He is the commentator who forces action, who won't allow the others to fall back into the darkness of a simpler and, therefore, more comfortable world.

During their travels through the worlds, the first beings of the Navajo encounter all kinds of adventures. There is the great flood brought on by Coyote. There is the great discord between men and women; women seeking their own sex for love-gratification; the birth of monsters who roam the Earth freely until, in the Fifth World, Changing Woman, symbol of life, is born. She gives birth to the Twin Slayers, who kill the monsters—their bodies now the lava-flows of Navajo land—thus bringing an end to male-female sexual disharmony. With the birth of Changing Woman, the emergence is complete. Her beneficent creature-power is the strongest of any of the Holy Ones, including First Man. A Blessing Way (healing ceremony to promote inner harmony) is given for her, and the Holy People go to their home in the Nadir, leaving the Earth to the new race born from Changing Woman's body: Diné, The People.

MEDITATION ON
EMERGENCE Part II

"Before the hump-backed bear with blue eyes was ever sat upon" refers to the bear from a sand painting used in the Mountaintop Way. Sand paintings are intricate dry paintings done on the floor of the hogan for curative purposes. The patient sits upon the painting as part of the cure: he draws strength from it and is psychically reborn.

Holy People and animals emerge from the underworld at the same time. Animals and insects have magical powers *and* human characteristics: thus Coyote is trouble-causer; Wolf, thief. Most animals are positive forces referred to as Brother and Sister, members of the same family as ours.

The last stanza describes some of the ritual which must be undergone when a person has died and the body must be disposed of. The number four is repeated in Navajo ritual. There are four directions, four seasons, four colors, four sacred mountains. White and white shell are east; blue and tortoise, south; yellow and coral, west; black and jet, north. Other magic numbers are five and nine.

Coyote is present here as the eternal trickster and trouble-causer. But his mischief is a dualism, bringing the dangerous and negative flood, but, because of the flood, forcing the People into a more complex and promising world.

Corn is the most important crop to the Navajo and to other western Indians. Originating in the New World, it is the only primary grain (the others being rice and wheat) which has to be cultivated. Sacred and lifegiving, corn pollen is sprinkled on patients during healing chants; corn meal is eaten in the marriage ceremony; corn pollen and corn meal are used in prayer blown on the wind for prayers.

The mountains are the four sacred mountains which border the Navajo lands; Mount Blanco (Sisnaajini) to the east; Mount Taylor (Tsoodzil) to the south; the San Francisco peaks (Doko'oosliid) to the west; and Mount Hesperus (Dibentsaa) to the north.

Younger Sister
and Blue Racer Snake

The Younger Sister was very tired,
her moccasins worn thin,
her clothing in rags.

She could see smoke from Great Snake's
smoke-pipe close behind her.

She ran until she came to a place
called Sage Canyon.
There she almost stepped upon
a slender young man with a bluish face,
sunning himself on a rock.

"I am called Blue Racer," he said
"Where are you going in such a hurry?"

"I am being chased by Great Snake," she said.

"No Great Snake comes here,"
he laughed confidently.
"Take off your ragged clothes
and come with me."

She went to the young man naked
and he blew into a tiny hole
four times
until it was large enough
for both to enter.

When Great Snake came to the place

where the Younger Sister
had shed her clothes,
he grabbed them up in his mouth
and hissed:
"Oh, my wife! My wife!"

But Blue Racer spoke through the tiny hole,
which was too small
for Great Snake to enter,
and told him to go away.

The power of his words
was too much for Great Snake
and he was forced to turn around
and go home.

That night, Blue Racer dressed
in his finest snake's skin
and came forward
to meet Younger Sister,
who wished at that moment
to go outside.

She tried to leave, but a throng of snakes
blocked her path;
they were on all sides of her,
so she threw herself
on the ground.

Next morning, the snake people
complained bitterly.
One said: "Sister-in-law is not kind,

she stepped on my neck."
Another said: "She stepped on my arm."
And another: "She hurt my leg."

Later, she had a pain in her stomach;
they gave her medicine
and she was quiet

Then came her children:
a boy-child snake
and a girl-child snake.

And that is why when we see
a snake crawling on the ground
or sunning itself on a rock,
we call it by name,
and send it gently away.

MEDITATION ON
YOUNGER SISTER AND BLUE RACER SNAKE

It is said that the Snake People intermarried not only with the Navajo but with other Native American tribes. Blue Racer is both man and snake—simultaneously. Encircling the helpless girl, the multiple folds of his blue coils master her and they make love. The boy-child snake and the girl-child snake are offspring of this union—with all the problems inherent in such a union. The human dilemma of the story lies in the difficulties not of sex, but of marriage. It is, for instance, the in-laws who make trouble for the couple, just as they sometimes do in "normal" human marriages. The resolution, though, as in many of the stories in this book, is harmony: "man" is no more master of snake than snake is master of "man." Together, they share an innocent kingdom.

Shiprock

The Utes were after him and Young Man was fearful. He came to a river and the water lifted and Young Man went under it to the home of Otter. Otter said: "The enemy will not come here. You are safe."

The Utes searched the country but they could not find Young Man. So he left the home of Otter and moved into a new country and again he grew fearful that the Utes had found his track. As he ran, he cried and someone called to him from a tree. A round voice said: "Why do you cry?"

Young Man answered: "The Utes are after me. They want my scalp."

The voice said: "Come up here, Grandchild. They will not follow you here."

Young man climbed the tree and he entered the home of Owl. Owl circled the tree four times and he sprinkled sun-medicine to hide Young Man. The Utes hunted around and around the tree but they found nothing and finally went away.

Young Man set out to find his home country, but he traveled very far out of his way and moved in circles so he was lost, with tears in his eyes, when he heard someone speak to him.

This time White Ground Squirrel called to him and lifted up a greasewood bush and blew four times under it. Then he went down into the hole and Young Man followed and was soon safe from his enemies, the Utes, but after he came out of the hole he got lost again in another strange country. As his eyes filled with tears, he heard a small voice coming from under the rocks: "Why do you cry?" it asked.

"Because the Utes are after my scalp."

This time Mountain Rat spoke to Young Man. "Never mind," it said. "They never enter my house." And he quickly opened his home under the rocks and Young Man passed through, and the rocks were sealed in place.

Again the Utes searched all over, and again they did not find him. After the Utes went away, Young Man came out into the sun and walked very far. He reached the San Juan River and the water was high. He walked along the river-bank, eating berries that grew there. He heard someone behind him.

A voice said: "Grandson, what are you doing here?" Young Man turned and looked into the face of Man of Dark Color.

"I have come far," he answered, "from the country of the Utes. I am trying to reach my home, but the river is high and I cannot cross."

"Shall I take you across?" said Man of Dark Color. Young Man climbed on his back.

When the two had crossed the San Juan River safely and Young Man had been put down gently, Man of Dark Color turned into a black rock that grew and grew, while his arms spread out into great wings. He is there to this day: The Rock with Wings, *Shiprock*.

MEDITATION ON
SHIPROCK

The Utes often traded, intermarried, and made war with the Navajo. Their country, forming the old northernmost border of Navajo land (on the "other side" of the San Juan River), was "enemy territory." Shiprock, standing high on the plains, is the sign that the Navajo boy in the poem is well within his own country. On a spiritual plane, the poem deals with intercessory helpers. It is not just Young Man's totem animal who protects him, but a pantheon of good-spirit animals. In facing Man of Dark Color without fear, the young man is borne across the river to safety. At the same time, his protector becomes the permanent guardian of all the People—Shiprock.

Whistle

At first the man rubbed
yucca fruit and sacred waters
over the woman's heart.
Then she did the same to him,
and this was good
except jealousy came
from somewhere
and man and woman
were kept apart.

A medicine was prepared,
which made man and woman
whistle between the legs.

After that, they were together again
and the whistle's pitch was different.

That is why a boy's voice
and a girl's voice are not the same:
that is why voices change
and other things happen,
over and over.

MEDITATION ON
WHISTLE

It is said that one in anger cannot whistle. Whistling, therefore, is not a sound of sadness, anger, or depression, but that of spirit, the true spirit of things, singing. In this Navajo version of Adam and Eve, it is jealousy rather than guilt or curiosity that conspires to upset the balance of Navajo Eden. Acceptance, the embracing of the cycle of life, is apparent in the difference in the whistle-pitch and things happening "over and over." It is also significant that the whistle, voice or speech of man and woman, comes from that most vital place where all true speech may be said to originate—between the legs. Or to put it another way: the voice of sex, the presence of that which you are in presence of that which you aren't: harmony.

Growing Old

First Man and First Woman
did what was best
for the Sky, the Earth, and The People.
But after Coyote's bad conduct
their work went sour

This is how it goes:
The People's hair was supposed
to remain black like the crow,
but one day there came
a bird-person with white head,
whose name was Nuthatch.

He spoke: "Grandchildren,
look here, I am turning grey;
I am growing old."

When he flew away
the dust of his wings
fell upon The People's hair
and they knew there was such a thing
as old age.

But The People's teeth
were still white, and strong, and clean—
First Man and First Woman
had made it so:
white teeth for white corn.

One day, Old Man Gopher
came with face

all puffed out in pain.

"Oh, Grandchildren," he groaned,
"I have a toothache,
pull my bad teeth for me."

So The People pulled his bad teeth
until only the two front ones
were left.
And from that time on,
The People knew what it was like
to have a toothache.

That is why The People
now wear the top feathers
of the Nuthatch
and have grey hairs;
and that is why
they rub their cheeks
when Old Man Gopher
pops out of his hole.

MEDITATION ON
GROWING OLD

"Growing Old" may be viewed as a Navajo version of Adam and Eve expelled from the Garden of Eden. Coyote's "bad conduct" or mischievous nature—the stealing of Water Monster Babies in The Flood—however, is still a far cry from The Serpent's attempt to unseat God's love of humankind. Coyote can be seen as devilish, but is more accurately pictured here as a divine trickster whose morality lessons are The People's own. Deities and members of the human race are not differentiated. Aging, then, is not a loss of innocence as much as it is a necessary attainment of wisdom. Grey hair and the rubbing of cheeks—that which Diné accept because "this is how it goes," "that is why," that is the story of it. There is humor in this acceptance that Old Man Gopher and the Grandchildren *share*, that animals and men are heir to the misdeeds of Coyote, the mirthful misdoer who must learn, more than once, the meaning of life so that others may share in the balance.

Visit of the Holy Person

"I was sitting here today
when suddenly everything turned
bright white inside the hogan.
I turned and saw a handsome man.
He asked about you, my son.
I told him you stay away
all day because the girls tease you.

He asked what we ate
and where we slept.
I showed him the seed cakes I made
and the rabbits you killed.
I showed him our woven mat beds.
Then he reached out
for a piece of bread and he spoke:
"This is my food also."

As soon as he said this,
he was gone
and there was nothing
left of him
except the piece of seed cake
and a single track
outside the door."

MEDITATION ON
VISIT OF THE HOLY PERSON

Of significance is the line: 'This is my food also.' Whatever life may separate that which we know from that which we do not, there is, or may be, the inevitable sharing of appetite. This is the appetite of life on either side of the division of death. The world of divinity participates also in the daily acts of life, the simple movements of hand to mouth and body to bed. Those things we do, they do. There is a correspondence between the earthly appetites of the Greek gods and those of the Navajo. Both find themselves attracted in various ways to mortals.

Rainbow

When I cross Deep Canyon
with nowhere for a belly
and nothing for a heart
I seek my friend, Rainbow.
I walk soft as a young deer
on Rainbow's rain-colored road.

MEDITATION ON
RAINBOW

The canyon's belly and the canyon's heart are fed by the same universal emptiness we find in Taoist writings. Rainbow is a spiritual ally and the man or woman who knows this must become a deer, "soft" and "young," in order to make use of the incorporeal power of radiant moisture-light in the atmosphere, rainbow.

Turquoise Horse

I am the Sun's son.
I sit upon Turquoise Horse
at the opening of the sky.

My horse walks on terrifying hooves
and stands on the upper circle of the rainbow
with a sunbeam in his mouth
for a bridle.

My horse circles all the peoples of the Earth.

Today, I ride on his broad back
and he is mine;
Tomorrow he will belong to another.

MEDITATION ON
TURQUOISE HORSE

On a literal level, we may envision the non-indigenous horse as a Navajo symbol of access to a world of power and transformation. However, when viewed spiritually, Turquoise Horse is man's birthright of freedom and masculine ascension. The Sun's son rides upon his back and all things are joined—rainbow, sunbeam bridle, circle of people. Selfishness and personal glory are overcome by the sharing of the turquoise horse: "Tomorrow he will belong to another."

COYOTE

When he reached the hogan of Coyote Lady
he threw the trophies at her feet.

I
HOW COYOTE GOT HIS YELLOW EYES
A Traditional Tale

One day Coyote was trotting along an arroyo watching his shadow when suddenly he looked up and saw Magpie cackling at him.

"What's so funny, Magpie? Speak up 'cause I haven't time to waste on the likes of you!"

"That so?" Magpie said, and he grinned his broadest grin and cackled his sickest cackle.

Now there's no bird in all the deserts of the West who can look down his beak at other animals as well as brother Magpie. With his great long black-and-white tail, his cocky eye, and lofty opinion of himself, he's hard to beat—even Buzzard'll look the other way when he passes Magpie in a tree.

"This is no time for smart-ass manners," said Coyote. "I know your silly habit of staring down at people, so why don't you fly off and mind your own business?"

"Such a temper!" said Magpie, polishing his beak on his blue satin jacket. "And to think," he added, "that I was going to teach you a fabulous trick. Well, some other day."

"Wait," said Coyote. "What trick?"

By and by, Magpie dropped from his perch and strutted upon the ground like the high-class salesman that he is.

"Now, let us see. . .ah, yes, Brother Coyote, let me ask you this: did I ever show you the game of Throw-Away-Eyes?"

"You didn't," answered Coyote, and he began to drool at

the promise of such a game. "How is it done? Tell me."

"Like this!" said Magpie and, without another word or gesture, he tucked himself into the air, twirled his head, and tossed both his eyes into the wind. But, of course, Magpie was quick as summer lightning, and though he was blind, he flew right to where his two eyes were falling, caught them up safely, and flew back down to Coyote.

"What do you think of *that*, Brother Coyote?" he asked, preening his wind-ruffled feathers.

Coyote wasn't listening. He was off on a trot of his own, throwing his head in the air like Magpie had done, trying to lose his eyes and catch them again. But he was not at all successful, and Magpie, seeing how badly he was doing, chuckled and flew along beside him.

"Not like *that*! Like *this*!" And Magpie did the trick over again so that Coyote might get it right.

Coyote was one animal who never paid attention to anyone unless that anyone was himself. So he ignored Magpie's coaching, which was a great mistake, for very shortly he got the knack of it—learned to toss his eyes up into the sky, but *not* how to get them back in again. Soon he was stone-blind in the desert sun.

"Magpie, where are you? Come help me!" he begged. "I've lost my eyes!"

But Magpie had other business to attend to and he had flown off some time ago. Coyote sat all by himself and he couldn't see his shadow, because now everywhere was shadow. Dark, dark shadow. Coyote was miserable without his eyes.

"What'll I do now?" he said aloud. "What'll I do now?"

Just then Nuthatch flew by. He saw Coyote and took pity on him. How sad, he thought: Brother Coyote the trickster, minus his tricks.

"Listen here," said Nuthatch, "I've known you to do good things for people now and then. If I get back your eyes, will you promise to hole up for a while and lay off the rest of us?"

"I promise to be as good as Hummingbird," said Coyote—and it didn't matter a bit to him that he was lying.

Nuthatch flew over to a piñon tree and pecked at the bark with his little beak and flew back to Coyote and sat on his nose.

"Here, from now on you'll have eyes of piñon gum, nice bright yellow eyes!"

Nuthatch put them in place and Coyote could see the mesas and arroyos and peaks, the pink and yellow hills, the turquoise sky. He could see it all, and that made him so happy, so very happy that he was on his way without so much as thanks or goodbye.

"Hey, Coyote, don't go near a fire, or your new eyes will melt," Nuthatch said.

But Coyote didn't hear a word because now that he had his new eyes, he was already running off looking for lunch. And presently he found it, a campfire with a couple of Prairie Dogs roasting piñon nuts.

"Roast Prairie Dog!" slavered Coyote to himself, and he came up to the fire and pretended to show interest in the nuts.

"Coyote doesn't eat nuts," squealed Prairie Dog, and he and his friends stepped to the other side of the fire. "Help yourself, they're already popping out of the coals."

Coyote wanted to fool the stupid Prairie Dogs, so he made as if he were fishing about with his paws for the roasted nuts.

"Don't get them out with your paws; anyone can do it like that. Use your tongue the way we do," said Prairie Dog.

Coyote snatched at the roasted piñon nuts and got a burnt tongue. He was about to cool it off when someone turned out the lights. Too late to stop his eyes from melting, he ran into the wind as fast as he could go. This cooled him out, but not before the melted piñon gum ran alongside his nose and made those two famous streaks which every Coyote born into this world will always have, along with the bright yellow eyes that look just like piñon gum.

II
Coyote in Love

Long ago there lived a Coyote Lady, who was the sister of twelve divine brothers. She had many handsome suitors but none could win her.

One day Ma-i, the Coyote, thought he would see if the stories of her beauty were true. So he trotted across hills and valleys to her hogan. When he saw her his eyes grew large and he said without thinking, "What must I do to win your paw?"

"It would be of no use for you to know; you couldn't satisfy me."

Coyote believed there was nothing in the world he couldn't do. "Tell me," he said, "what?"

"All the others have failed. How could you succeed?"

Coyote would not give up. A third time he asked, "Tell me what I must do to win your paw?"

She repeated, "You cannot win my paw. You are not big enough, strong enough, or sexy enough."

"Tell me," said Coyote desperately, "I'll do anything."

Now the fourth time he asked, Coyote Lady answered, "The person who marries me must first kill a giant."

So Coyote went away and devised a plan. The next day he started out to find a giant. After a short time he met Grey Giant, who was half as big as Big Pine, with an evil eye and long yellow tusks for teeth.

"Grey Giant," Coyote shouted, "do you know why you can't catch your enemies? You can't run fast enough. I can jump over four bushes in one bound." Coyote jumped over four sage bushes to show off.

"Cousin Coyote," said Grey Giant, "how is it that you run so good?"

"I'll tell you the secret, but first you build a sweat-house so we can purify ourselves."

"All right, Cousin, I'll build the sweat-house." And Grey Giant set to work carrying logs and putting them up tent-fashion and plastering the chinks with mud.

Coyote went off and hunted until he found the thigh bone of an antelope that Mai-t'so, the wolf, had killed and eaten. He hid it under his fur coat. When he returned, the sweat house was finished, so he and Grey Giant built a fire and heated rocks and made a leaf carpet for the floor. Coyote hung the four blankets of the sky over the doorway—one white, one blue, one yellow, and one black. It made the sweat house dark inside. They took off their clothes and hung them with their weapons on Big Pine; then they entered the sweat house and sat down.

"Now," said Coyote, "do as I say and you will become a fast runner. Cut the flesh of your thigh to the bone, and then break the bone; I will cut mine first to show you how."

"Don't it cause pain?" asked Grey Giant, stupidly.

"That part is soon over," said Coyote. "And afterward you'll be a fast runner." Then Coyote reached for a great stone knife and pretended to whack off his thigh.

He howled and he yowled, so that the sweat-house shook with the vibrations. "Agh! What pain!" he hollered. And he prayed and sang and pretended to slash his leg some more.

It was dark in the sweat house and Grey Giant couldn't see a thing. Coyote put the old bone on top of his thigh and thrust it toward Grey Giant.

"There, you can feel my bone laid bare. Feel it with your hand."

Grey Giant put his hand on Coyote's leg and felt the antelope bone that Coyote had smuggled into the lodge.

"True. You cut to the bone."

"I do it often to make myself a fleet runner," said Coyote. "Now comes the worst part. I have to bust my bone." He held the stone knife above his head and brought it down with all his strength. Crack! The bone splintered into pieces. Coyote howled and prayed.

"Feel it, Grey Giant, feel it!"

Grey Giant felt the broken ends which had scattered on the floor. "What you say is true, Cousin, but don't it hurt bad?"

"Yes," gagged Coyote. "But it's why I'm the fastest runner in the world." Coyote spit on his thigh and sang: "Tohe! Tohe! Tohe! Heal together! Grow together! Tohe! Tohe! Tohe! In a short time he said, "Grey Giant, feel my leg. It is well. I can run faster than ever now."

Grey Giant felt the leg all over. "I will do as you have done. I too want to be a fast runner."

"Here's the knife," said Coyote, and Grey Giant took the stone knife and began to cut away the skin on his thigh. He howled like thunder. "Never mind if it hurts," said Coyote. "Just keep right on cutting."

Grey Giant roared and howled but he kept on cutting until—scratch!—he reached bone. "Cousin, I am now to the bone."

"Break the bone," said Coyote. Grey Giant gave his leg a mighty whack with the stone knife. The bone cracked, shattered into pieces.

"It is done," roared Grey Giant, and he commenced to pray and sing as Coyote had done. He held the two parts of the leg together. "Tohe! Tohe! Tohe! Heal together! Grow together! Tohe!

Tohe! Tohe! Help me, Coyote. Help me, Cousin. The bone won't heal."

Coyote saw that it was time for him to leave. He ran out of the sweat house and fetched his bow and arrows. He took away the sky blankets from the door and shot four arrows into Grey Giant, who fell to the floor and died.

Coyote cut off his scalp with the stone knife and hung it on the end of a cedar stick. Giants are the only people in Navajo country with yellow hair and Coyote knew that Coyote Lady would recognize Giant's scalp. But, to make sure, he took Giant's great quiver and arrows for further proof of his cunning act.

When he reached the hogan of Coyote Lady, he threw the trophies at her feet: the yellow-haired scalp, the great quiver, the arrows. "I have killed Grey Giant. Now for my reward. Marry me!" said Coyote.

"Not yet. You have not done *all* that I require."

"What more?" Coyote whined.

"The man who marries me must die four times and come to life."

"You speak the truth? You mean if I die four times and come to life you will marry me?"

"Yes," replied Coyote Lady absently.

"You promise not to think up new tasks for me to do?"

"That is all I ask."

Four times Coyote asked the same question and when she gave the same answer the fourth time he said, "Now you can kill me."

She led him outside her hogan and told him to lie down. Then she took a heavy club and hit him over the head. She beat him on the back and on the legs and all over his body until he was thoroughly crushed. Only the tip of his nose and the tip of his tail were untouched.

"Coyote is dead," she laughed, throwing down her club. And she returned to the hogan for she had much work to do. Later that day while she was weaving, she saw someone come to the doorway of her hogan. She looked up, and there she saw the figure of Coyote.

"I've won the first time," he said. "Three more times I die, and then I claim you for my wife."

Coyote Lady did not say anything, but again she went outside the hogan and picked up a big club. She bade him lie down and again she beat Coyote to a pulp. This time she picked up the pieces of his body, threw them in all directions, and went inside to resume her weaving. Once more he was standing in the doorway, as if he had never been beaten to a pulp and thrown in all directions.

"Now I've won two games. If I win twice more, you're my wife."

Coyote Lady took no chances the third time. She beat Coyote until he was nothing but flayed fur and the wind had blown him in the four earthly directions. Luckily for Coyote, she had neglected to crush the tip of his tail and the tip of his nose. It was some time before he could get himself together again, but he was by no means dead, and by evening he came round a third time and grinned in Coyote Lady's face.

Now she was truly afraid, because no living thing could withstand her beatings, and Coyote always came back good as new. The fourth time she mashed him with a cornmeal masher, ground him into meal, and, satisfied that he was finally done for and she was free to marry someone with more sex appeal, she went inside to finish her weaving.

It took Coyote the longest time of his life to pull himself together this last time, but he succeeded as before, because his nose-tip and the tip of his tail were intact and unharmed.

When Coyote Lady looked up to see the moon, she

thought she saw Coyote standing in it, his head and shoulders all silvery and smooth. "Coyote, is that you?" she asked fearfully, not believing what she saw.

Coyote stepped down from the ridge wearing a mantle of moonlight on his fur, and he said two words. "I win."

MEDITATION ON
COYOTE IN HIS OWN WORDS

"Everyone tells stories on me, Coyote. Wherever I go I hear I did this or that or the other. But these stories are never what happened—they're what somebody wanted to happen because one of The People was making a story and a lesson had to be put in. I would tell The People this (and with all due respect, they are not the ones who created me; I created myself long ago in the time of the coming out of the earth)—I would tell them that I am not a rascal, wrong-doer, mischievous person. I am not wholly a person and I am not merely an animal. I am both of these things or more. I am not a deity either. Let me see if I can explain.

Sometime in the future the world will come to an end. Again. It has happened before. I can see clearly now, as I tell you this, that I will be around while some of you will not. As I see it, I will be doing what I always like to do: scrounging around looking for food. Now, because there is no essential difference between past, present and future, I will say this to you the way it happened, the way it will happen, and the way it happens. . . .

I am down at the dump, rummaging. I don't know how much is left of that world over the horizon. It went white and red last night and it was like the time of the Great Flood, the bands of color like the four directions, like the sacred shells and stones of the universe: red coral, black coral, white abalone, turquoise. I saw the light go off and I knew you were at it again. This is what gets me angry. My reputation is always being ruined by the things you do that you decide to blame on me. It is easier that way, I know. Well, you go ahead and do what you please—you will, anyway.

But as I was saying. The sky made the colors of the four sacred peaks. And then all was dim and dark.

I see the end of the world.
I see it coming.
I know it won't end.
I know I make it up,
I know I am the storyteller of it.
I know you did it
with your garbage dumps
and your sirens
and your too-thick sick
concentrations of your kind
with your living on top of your selves
with no room to breathe
and the things that don't taste
good anymore
but I eat anyway
because that's my job
and the air I used to breathe
that doesn't taste good anymore
because you make it smell
with your smokes
and your hoax.

I am the deliverer of these truths
I know what I say is true
since you have always

appointed me Head Man—
you wouldn't have any stories
without me, would you?

So I go into town knowing that you won't be there anymore. I walk right up Main Street, step into a tobacco shop and, there being no one present to say yes or no, I go behind the counter and pick out the most expensive cigar. Everything smells different now, but the smoke is good. I don't have anyone to talk to but Cockroach. He was around in the old days when you said I started the first hullaballoo, but he didn't talk much then, and he talks even less now.

Now I went and got me the best suit in town. My cigar was half smoked by then. The pants were too baggy—I have big thighs and skinny calves. But the jacket looked great. I walked out to the Plaza and smoked down my cigar. There was no one to look at how good I looked. Cockroach and his People were too busy eating to pay attention, and I hate it when he talks with his mouth full.

The rain, so soon.
Winter wet sleek rain
in summer noon.
Rain is rain
but this again, so soon.

And wind, so soon.
Winter thunder hard cloud
in summer noon.
Thunder is thunder
but this again, so soon.

I will wear my new suit out into the weather. Badger will see me and we will get drunk again on juniper wine. How to tell Badger there's no more world for us to revel in? No one will see me in my new Pendleton too-hot wool shirt. I have a winter felt with two earholes cut out for my big listening-ears. No one will see it. No one will know—

> for a long, long time.
> For too long a time.
> For days to come
> and days gone by
> no one will know.

If you want to get right down to it, that's what rankles my ass. No one knowing me in my own home town."

BLUE-EYED BEAR

The sick person has vision of Bear
when he sits upon painted sand.

Blue-Eyed Bear

Inside the hogan
colored earths make bear tracks
lead in,
bear tracks and sunlight—
sun dogs
at the four quarters.
Bear is soaked in sunlight
in the center.
Twigs at the entrance of Bear's den
are trees.

The sick person has a vision of Bear
when he sits upon painted sand.
Then Bear-man
rushes into the hogan, snarling and growling.
All the sitting people join in—
this is the moment
when the women faint.

MEDITATION ON
BLUE-EYED BEAR

This poem refers to the Mountaintop Way, which literally translated means "a chant towards a place within the mountains." Since bears live in the mountains, they are the major power in the Mountaintop Way.

The Navajos have a strong fear of the power of the bear. In spite of mythological references to his being good (he and Snake Man were guardians of Sun's house, protectors of Changing Woman, and were given by Changing Woman to The People to guard them on their journeys) he also must be considered potentially dangerous. After having done much good for The People, he began to cause coughs and bad luck and aligned himself with evil. Because of this, he and his relatives were assigned to walk in Black Mountain where, ever since, there have been a lot of bears.

Many chants have an accessory rite known as "the shock rite." It is referred to in this poem when Bear Man enters and "the women faint." The purpose of this shock rite is to correct symptoms caused by the contemplation of the supernatural. Bear Man represents dangers and sufferings and his effect is intended to eliminate fear and inspire confidence.

The purpose of the Mountaintop Way is to remove all bad effects caused by bears. It is to cure disease, invoke unseen powers on behalf of The People for rain and good crops, and to perpetuate harmony. By sitting on the sand painting described in the poem, the sick person draws strength and is healed.

The Mountaintop Way can be celebrated only in the winter when thunder is silent and the rattlesnake is hibernating. To relate the tales at any other time would bring death from lightning or a snake bite.

White Man's Ghost

White man's ghost which threatens
    my clouds.
White man's ghost which knows
    no resting place.
White man's ghost which comes
    and goes on skittery feet,
pawing at my body places:
       my suns, my spruces, my clouds.

I will wear now those dark flints
that protect,
I will dance as they rattle
upon my skin.

The dark bear: I borrow the flints
of his furred hands;
the soaring eagle: I borrow the flints
of her feathered hands.

Now I will wash my body's house
in the pollen that rests on blue ponds.
A fine yellow pollen, water pollen
makes my skin shine,
makes my heart great
so that the white man's ghost
will no longer threaten
my suns, my spruces, my clouds.

MEDITATION ON
WHITE MAN'S GHOST

Ghosts of the dead may cause harm to the living, especially if the living offended the dead person sometime before the death occurred. Ghosts wander at night bringing physical illness, misfortune, mental anguish, all as forms of revenge. The Enemy Way is needed to rid the victim of the power of the ghost. (See "Stargazer" in this book.) In the poem, fear of the white man, perhaps murdered by the speaker, is threatening him; ritual steps must be taken to exorcise the evil spirit. On yet another level, the white man's ghost refers to the alien culture which has threatened and continues to threaten the Navajo.

Cornfather-Dancer's Headdress

Go find the hide of a deer not killed by a weapon. Draw the cutting-lines for the skin with a piece of crystal. Use the sinew from the right side of the spinal column for sewing the right side of the headdress. Yellow feathers from the little yellow bird are sewn on the right side and the whole work is done by a righthanded man.

Now for the left, use the sinew from that side of the spinal column. A lefthanded man will sew bluebird feathers on the left side of the headdress.

The right-side feathers are for the Black Water Jar which brings rain. The left-side feathers are for the ears of Corn. The dancer with the headdress is called Corn Father.

MEDITATION ON
CORNFATHER-DANCER'S HEADDRESS

Right and left refer back to the Twin Slayers, sons of Changing Woman. The bold, right side (representing the Sun Father) is the masculine twin, the one who takes the initiative in legendary encounters. The left side (representing Earth, Mother, Moon) is the more subtle of the two and more shy; he walks to the left, the heart side. (This sense of polarity is beautifully expressed in Frank Waters' *Masked Gods*.) As in Jungian thought, unity or harmony of the individual self is brought about by knowledge of these two aspects of the self.

The First Frost of Autumn

Between the first frost of autumn
and the third moon of winter

something lives between:
it has eyes that hear,
ears that see.

With beads and waters and pollens
it breathes, sings, dances—

it lives
between
like a knife
stuck in a rock.

None may go unclean
between
the haunted breath of autumn
the second wind of winter.

MEDITATION ON
THE FIRST FROST OF AUTUMN

The Winter Ceremonies, which last about four months, cannot be celebrated in summer when snakes, bears, and lightning are prevalent. They begin when the ground freezes in October. This is a time of renewed balance and circular harmony; the winter stories begin, the summer stories are over. Traditional Navajos walk softly on the first snow, for it is Changing Woman's change of dress. The alive time of between is a cautious time, a time of seeing without the eyes, of hearing without the ears. "None may go unclean" means that none may forget the ritual exchange in the between-time, the moment when all of nature looks inward and feels change, a time of turning. None may omit, therefore, the rite of passage into the coming of winter.

Winter Thunder

Winter thunder
makes my separate parts
scatter.

First, my breath is gone, caged and rasping
by old willows,
then my bones and teeth
are blown to the twelve winds!
My ribs gone, my pelvis, my spine,
my collarbone, my tailbone—
sadly do I lose my bones!

My saliva and hair is gone, buried
in dry lizard rocks!
My skin, blasted, ripped
by forks of lightning!

My vitals, my spleen, my liver—
all but my heart—blown and spiked
on cactus thorns.
I see them there, but cannot touch them.
I must call them back,
I must beckon their return
with gifts of pollen.

In several whirlwinds they come back:
when I stand in the center of my broad cornfield
beautified with white corn, yellow corn,
with corn pollen, with grasshoppers
and the hundred corn-carrying beetles.

My parts return to me through the tips of my fingers.
They return to their place of birth,
they enter the round cave that is me.
My bones and teeth and saliva
and hair and skin . . .
all return, all forgiven, all given back.

And I ask of them: did you like the Places of the Night
where Winter Thunder took you and shook you,
before you came home?

And my bones refuse to answer.

MEDITATION ON
WINTER THUNDER

This poem suggests the long and involved Flint Way, where the hero seduces the wife of White Thunder, who later shatters him with a bolt of lightning. According to the story, Gila Monster is the singer who restores the hero by cutting his own body into tiny pieces and throwing them in all directions; and then is restored by the Wind People, Sunlight People, and other Holy People. (Dismemberment and reintegration also are illustrated in the Coyote chapter of this book. The effect of weather, out of harmony with man, appears in the meditation in that section.) In healing himself, he restores the shattered hero.

The Man

Man who walks when dog will
    not bite him.
Man who cups stars in his palms.
Man whose bare feet are tickled
    by snakes' tongue. . .

"This Man, I call him,
I have need of him.
Bring him to me, for I am sick
and will die unless he comes
and tells me what is ailing.
His medicine is strong,
he will tell me if I live or die."

A lamb was given in exchange
and Man-Who-Looks-Into-Sun
came to look at a young girl.
He stared directly
into the heart of a star and sang.
He kept looking at that star.
Then it broke open
before his eyes
and he saw a blazing hogan
come out of it.

"That means the girl will die."
And in less than one month
    she was dead.

Man who walks with stars drawn
upon his skin.

Man whose hands are early blessed
        by pollen.
Man who sees no one trapped
        in the sun.

"Man, O, Man
I have need of you,
for I am another
about to die.
Come, sing me well,
        come sing me!"

A lamb was given
and another's daughter was visited
by the Man.
He sat quiet by folds
of moonwhite sheep fur
and stared into the girl's eyes.

"Tonight, a white sign comes around
the hogan like frost;
that means she will be well
within a week."
        And she was.

"Man who is brother of white winds
and black fogs,
I have strewn sands in your hogan
and eaten pollen-balls made by your hands;
but my hands do not move
when I gaze and sing:
does that mean I may never see signs?"
        The Man answered "Yes."

The Chanter's Failure

When the Night Chant fails nine times,
I step into a piñon fire
made by my own hands
in a moth's trance,
and splash my bones
     with fiery blue water—.

Only when the flames
have blackened me clean
will the ash of guilt
blow far, far away
from my grandfather's
     father's home.

Spirit Houses

made of dawns
made of moss
made of cottons
made of rain
made of suns
made of turquoise
made of winds
made of fur
made of pollens
made of flint
made of crystals

spirits of all houses under heaven,
bless my house made of mud, resin, pine.
bless my family made of blood, marrow, bone.

Prayer Before
The Night Chant
of "All is Well"

For long years I have kept
this beauty within me.
        It has been my life.
Now it is given
as the gift of dew is given by the sky
or the pollen from the cornflower.
My long days of those who listen
        be made longer.
I give so that no harm comes.
I make offerings
        of pollen
        of dew.

MEDITATION ON
MEDICINE WAYS

While herding his sheep, a Navajo herdsman was suddenly overcome by an acute headache. Returning to his hogan, he went to bed and a diviner was summoned to find the cause of the pain and what could be done for a cure. The diviner, an experienced hand-trembler, soon found the cause of the headache—an accidentally killed snake. A chant called the Evilway Chant was given by a singer and many relatives and friends came to join in the cure. At the end of five days, the man was well, his harmony restored.

Navajo ceremonies are centered around the maintenance of harmony (as in the Blessingway, used at the birth of a new baby, the change from girlhood to womanhood, or the blessing of a new hogan), or they are used, most commonly, to cure a person of a physical illness, a mental state, or bewitchment. Harmony and balance are essential to the Navajo; when a person has disturbed this harmony, even unknowingly, he or she will become ill. A cure can only occur through the proper ceremony (referred to as a chant, sing, or way), which, in retelling a portion of the Origin Story, symbolically recreates the world, and the patient. In such an exalted state, the patient slips free of past errors—for without error, there is no illness.

The Navajo view of sickness has many aspects. There is the symptom: the bad headache, the broken leg, the deep depression. There is also that which *caused* the illness: the broken taboo, the offended Holy People, the disruption of harmony. Treatment, to be effective, must deal with the illness beneath the illness. There are more than fifty chants or ways in Navajo ceremonials. Each is an intricate matrix of songs and rituals which must be carried out to perfection. A singer (or medicine man) who falters can bring evil or even death to a patient. Chants are so complicated that most singers will learn only one in a lifetime. Some of the ones used today are the Beautyway, the Windways, and the Holyways.

In each way, some portion of the Origin Story will unfold. The basic plot is usually that of a young man who leaves his home, often in search of adventure. During this search he—either knowingly or unknowingly—will go against the sanctions of the Holy People. As a result he is punished. To redeem himself, he must meet the demands of the Holy People and submit to a series of trials. Once these are fulfilled, the youth is taught by the Holy People songs which give him supernatural power. He then returns to his home where he is welcomed as the prodigal son, who teaches the new songs to his people. Afterwards, he chooses to live permanently with the Holy People.

Usually two skilled members of the tribe participate in the cure of a sick person. One is the diviner and the other is the singer, or medicine man. The diviner finds the cause of illness, which chant should be used as a cure, and which singer is best suited to carry out the ceremony. In Navajo there is no general word for diviner, but there is a word which means "that which he knows." Divining, common to most cultures, is the skill of gaining inner knowledge, or wisdom beyond the five senses. Those who have this ability are regarded as practitioners of prophecy: shamans.

Navajo diviners are divided into three categories: hand-tremblers, star (or sun) gazers, and listeners.* There are few Navajos today who are listeners, but hand-trembling and stargazing are still widely used. Someone having these skills, usually a man, may also be a singer, but this is not always the case. Diviners can be used to find lost articles or to identify witches, but most commonly they assist in cures. If a person is "wise enough," Navajos say, he or she will call for a diviner at the onset of illness. However, usually the diviner waits until a series of medicine men have tried and failed. Because of the complexity of illness, two medicine men may be prescribed by the diviner—one for obvious manifestation, one for underlying cause.

When a hand-trembler is called in, he will ask a small fee, generally no more than a few dollars. He washes his hands and forearms and, with one arm bared to the elbow, sits cross-legged near the patient. Sometimes he will sprinkle corn pollen on the patient and on his own bare arm. Except for the pollen, no other accessories, such as fetishes, are used.

Next, he says a prayer to the Gila Monster's spirit, asking for information about the sickness and its cure. The Gila Monster is thought to know everything and to see everything. It is he who taught hand-trembling to The People. They know this because his forefoot shakes when he lifts it in walking.

The prayer is followed by several minutes of singing. Dur-

---

*Listening as a means of diagnosing is rarely used among the Navajos today. Like stargazing, it must be learned. The ritual is conducted without the aid of sand paintings or fetishes; instead, the listener dips his finger into a powder made from the dried eardrum of a badger and puts a bit of this powder into his own ears. Taking another man with him, he goes outside the hogan and prays to "listening," to the power inherent in the act of it. He sings and then waits to "hear" the cause of the illness. Sounds are significant: the rattle of a rattlesnake, the roar of a bear, the crash of thunder. The sound of a person crying means that the patient will die.

ing the prayer, the diviner sits with eyes closed; at the beginning of the singing, his hand begins to shake. The diviner thinks of diseases, chants, medicine men and something ("that which he knows") tells him which ones are applicable. At this, the shaking stops, the ceremony finishes, and the diviner announces what he has learned. The source of disease may appear when a trembling hand travels over the body of the patient and, involuntarily, rests upon the afflicted spot. The proper medicine man is identified by the trembling hand pointing at his home. The proper chant comes when the hand of the diviner moves freely in the sand and prescribes the name of the chant.

Hand-tremblers have described the feeling which comes over their arm as similar to that of your hand falling asleep, a tingling sensation, a minor electric shock. This skill cannot be inherited or learned, but comes suddenly, like a gift.

Stargazing, unlike hand-trembling, can be learned from a practitioner of the art. The stargazer will go outside the hogan of the patient and sing to a star. When the star throws out a stream of light ("like a motion picture") the stargazer knows the cause of illness. White or yellow light, light directed on the hogan, indicates the patient will recover; red light means serious illness; if the hogan is shown as dark or burning, death is imminent. The light of the chosen star will point in the direction of the proper medicine man.

The singer or medicine man conducts the chant and does the actual healing. Highly trained by his apprenticeship to an elder singer, he must "live" his ceremony completely before he can help others.

A singer or medicine man must know all the songs of the chant perfectly: each story, each step in ritual. There is so much power in his knowledge that, if he makes a mistake, the patient may lose his life.

Because of the power which he holds, the medicine man is regarded with a certain amount of fear. He learns basic healing arts, hypnosis, massage, and such feats as pulling a bone from a patient's ear. Most important, however, is the trust he instills in his patient, giving the injured or sick person a feeling of confidence. When a medicine man loses his patient's trust, his career is finished.

During the healing ceremony, the relationship between the medicine man and the patient is very close. The patient also is "sung over," touched, painted, pollen-sprinkled, massaged. Whether it is a brief, one-day sing, or a full, nine-day sing, the two, medicine man and patient, are in a mutual state of oneness. The patient is surrounded by his family and friends, those who witness and share in his rebirth. This feeling of intimacy and sharing bonded by the ceremony is very important, for it restores the patient to the harmony of his family, as well as to the universal rhythm of life.

Once an old Navajo was asked why he still preferred going to medicine men rather than to the modern white doctors at the nearest hospital. His reply was that, in the hospital, the doctor hardly ever saw you, he barely touched you or talked to you. None of your family was present, and all you did was lie alone. In a Navajo ceremony, family, friends, and medicine man are together and the medicine man treats the whole body-mind rather than a part of either of them.

The sand painting, one of the most important aspects of a healing ceremony, is a dry painting made by the singer and his helpers on the clean-swept floor of the hogan. It is through this intricate and colorful design, made from colors which are sacred to the Navajo—black, red, yellow, white, and turquoise—that the Holy People are approached. The designs made in the sand paintings are traditional representations of the portion of the Origin Story which is being recited. There is a border around the painting, with an opening which, like the single thread leading out from the center of a Navajo blanket, is a symbolic exit, so that the Holy People cannot be trapped by the humans, nor the humans trapped with them.

During the course of the ceremony, the patient sits upon the sand painting while being "sung over." It is here, at this moment, that the patient is reborn with the universe, with Diné, and as an individual. After the ceremony, the sand painting is destroyed, the patient restored to "normal."

In the Navajo world, the present is most meaningful, for in a circle there is no beginning, no end, and the most important point is where you stand at the moment. Navajos do not concern themselves with life after death, nor do they spend the present preparing themselves for an afterlife. If they concern themselves with rules and rituals, it is because they do not want disruption of the harmony of the moment.

HEALINGS

As the long snake slipped into the protective ferns,
she heard its ten-rattled tail buzz one last time.

The Hand of Mary Tsosie

When Morning Girl was ten she knew she had something. At night her hands trembled like junipers in the wind.

She had watched her Aunt Mary Tsosie who was a hand-trembler. Her aunt was thought to be crazy by certain people in the tribe. Yet she was known as a hand-trembler and some people came to her for help with matters of the spirit, divorce, financial difficulties, or ill-health.

Once her Aunt Mary was boiling bitterweed for tea out in back of her hogan. A woman who was afraid her husband was a skinwalker came to her and asked what she should do. Mary Tsosie handed the woman some rosary beads and told her to count them with her thumb and forefinger, one by one, and to say "Hail Mary" softly to herself every time she counted off seven beads. She was to face the directions as she counted, moving octagonally, as the hogan is shaped to suit the cardinal points of the Navajo universe.

The woman did as she was told. And the boiling bitterweed tea of Mary Tsosie made clouds in the summer sky.

Morning Girl watched her aunt stirring, stirring. She observed that the strange afflicted woman turned and counted as the long wooden ladle of her aunt curved along the edges of the hundred-year-old iron kettle. The ladle in her aunt's hand would imitate the turning rounds of the rosary-bead-counting woman—clockwise, counter-clockwise, always going in the cardinal directions starting in the east, and rounding out the edges of the octagon.

Morning Girl observed these movements and understood them as she understood a white horse flicking flies on a hill. There was no separation between the understanding of what she saw and what she did not know she understood.

In an hour the stirring stopped and Morning Girl noticed that her Aunt Mary was standing, leaning slightly in the gentle southerly breeze that tickled the strands of loose hair about her cheekbones.

The hand that held the ladle was her left hand. It was beginning to shake, to tremble and, first quietly, then loudly, it began to make a distant sound of muffled thunder against the kettle's rounded lip. When that happened, her eyes lost focus and her face drained of blood, and Morning Girl knew Aunt Mary was in "the between place" where light, color, and sound lose definition but where things that may happen are seen truly before the events of nature give shape to them. Morning Girl knew the blank look of unshaped knowing that filled the hollows of her Aunt Mary's face.

Then the wind rustled and nipped the full pleated skirts of the two standing women, and it was done. But the afflicted woman never looked into the eyes of Mary Tsosie, but kept counting rosaries and saying Hail Marys under her breath, and the wind was one of evil portent. Morning Girl knew this without knowing why or how she knew this.

When the terrible vacancy went away, Mary Tsosie sat down, exhausted. Morning Girl had to help her. Her left hand still trembled, the fingers twitching like a dead rattlesnake that will not give up its spirit-tail. The hand of Mary Tsosie knew something more than her lips would say.

Late that evening she took some folded bills from the afflicted woman and said some words to her, and it was done.

Some months after, the woman who had paid for the hand-wisdom of Mary Tsosie caught fever and in her ninth month of pregnancy gave birth prematurely to a child with veiled eyes. A doctor had to cut the folds of skin away from them, and let the blood run cleanly down the child's face. The fingers were similarly joined or webbed, and incisions had to be made.

The spring that followed was very wet and the little toads of the desert that sing in wet times came out in numbers and sang loudly. One night while the afflicted woman was changing her child's diaper, a dark face appeared above the smoke-hole of her hogan. It was the furred face of her skinwalker husband come to do her harm. But the woman remembered what Aunt Mary Tsosie had told her to do: she whipped the urine-soaked diaper out of the baby's legs with a deft flick of her wrist and snapped it up the smoke-hole into the face of the surprised wolf.

The hot diaper burned his eyes and he coughed at the woman who, remembering Aunt Mary's words, pushed a pitcher of salt into the crackling fire. Blue flames shot up and a greasy smell of smoke belched up the smoke-hole into the howling face.

That was the last she ever saw of the wolf, her husband, though a Navajo wino in Flagstaff, who was said to make rain for tourists, died the following year from overexposure in a snow-storm. The lab report said that, in addition to hypothermia, the man had been suffering from salt poisoning.

The Prayer Tree

When her grandmother was dying, young Bessie did not know what to do. A centipede had bitten the old lady on the arm while she rolled in her sleep, and by noon that day her arm was as big around as her thigh. Bitterwater was the old lady's clan name, and her first name, like that of the granddaughter who was named after her, was Bessie.

In the evening the medicine man came. He bent over the woman only once and looked at the bite. Then he asked the family to shake out blankets and sheep furs and sweep the hard-packed floor of the summer hogan. Old Bessie Bitterwater moaned in a feverish sleep as they moved her outside into the starlight. Young Bessie helped her brothers, sisters, and mother shake out the blankets. Suddenly, in the bright firelight of juniper boughs, the medicine man whose white-given name was Sam Charlie, but who was better known on the reservation as Two Fats, stooped down and caught something with the sharpened stick he was flicking back and forth in his right hand.

Pinned and writhing under the fire-blackened stick was a fat green and ochre centipede. Two Fats had pierced its middle and its head bobbed and weaved like a snake. Harshly, he ordered young Bessie to stoke the fire and bring him four red-hot coals. One at a time, the girls took the smoking fire coals to the place where Two Fats squatted, puffing calmly on a corn-husk cigarette. When the fourth coal arrived, he dug a small concavity in the sand, put the coals into the little bed, ignited a juniper branch and blew the sweet smoke in the four directions. Then he took out his knife, sliced the furious centipede into four equal parts, and placed each one on the coals. The rancid smell of the wriggling creature sickened young Bessie.

Some minutes later, Two Fats removed the centipede husks, which were now delivered from the flame as a fine grey ash. This he put in the palm of his left hand, spat into it four times, and singing softly under his breath, mixed the centipede ash into a sticky paste.

Two fats took the paste over to where Bessie Bitterwater breathed fitfully in her sleep of troubled dreams. Making a small incision along the upper part of her right arm where the centipede venom had done its work—the skin all puffy and red—he sucked and spat the poison on the ground. After doing this he rubbed the paste from his left hand in a circular motion around the swollen place.

Long after Two Fats had gone home in his pickup truck, young Bessie watched over her grandmother. She knew that if old Bessie were to die, they would burn their summer hogan and sweep all tracks leading to it or away from it. Her burial place would be up in the rocks above the hogan where young Bessie had once found the gleaming burial jewelry of other elders. Washed free of its earthen home, exposed to the sun and rain, the glittering treasure was one which no Navajo would touch.

Young Bessie studied her grandmother's face. It did not look old. Her mother had had the same face, and she, in turn, saw herself in the facial mold which was unmistakably Bitterwater. When Bessie was five, her mother died of a sudden illness that caused her to shrink down to half her weight. The night she died, her grandmother took young Bessie out to dry wash behind the hogan where a single ponderosa grew in the barren flinty soil. How it survived with so little earth and such scant water, no one could say. Her grandmother showed young Bessie how to encircle the tree with her arms and hold it as if it were a loved one. The tree was round, she said, and holding it completed its roundness with the earth and the sky. This tree was a prayer tree, she said, its roots large and spreading as its branches—the two of equal roundness.

As you embraced the tree, the old woman said, you kept all that was round, safe. That was what she said. But young Bessie's mother died.

Now she held her arms around the tree again, for she knew that if her grandmother could not feel her arms, the prayer tree could, and some of its healing power would flow into the earth and into Bessie Bitterwater. She felt the frosty needles of the tree in her blood; she felt them carry an old song down under ground—from sun where power of life in heaven is stored, to earth where that power is joined. From needle to root, Bessie could feel herself share in the meeting of worlds, the bringing of harmony. She could feel the strength of Changing Woman waken in her heart and the clouds of darkness scatter from her mind.

At first light her grandmother opened her eyes and got up just as she had always done. She moved slowly and she did not speak to anyone, but she was quite alive. That afternoon the old woman washed her hair with yucca roots and went up into the burial rocks and sang a song. When young Bessie saw her in the light of early dusk, she saw also a small eagle feather in the first limb of the old ponderosa. Young Bessie wondered how many of these feathers her grandmother had offered to the wind. In the top branches of the prayer tree she saw the old feathers flying. One day her own daughter would put a feather in this tree; a feather for her, perhaps. She wondered if one day, when the tree was no longer there, the name Bitterwater would mean anything. But she knew that if she were no longer there herself, the tree, the clan would no longer matter. Now, the tree and its feathered family were a story only a few could read. One day, perhaps, there would be no tree to hang feathers on. Young Bessie looked at her grandmother who smiled back at her. They were alive, her eyes seemed to say, they were alive.

The Grandfather Chair

"Grandfather," Jimmy Blue Eyes said, "You promised you would not ride my horse until he was ready to ride."

The old man sat up straight in the hospital bed and looked as if he were about to ride the bed out the door and into the sky. He did not appear to be ready to die, and although his family had placed him there for that reason, he seemed unwilling to submit to their decision.

"I was just training him, Jimmy," the old man said. Then he laughed softly and a lot of wrinkles slid across his face. "But he ended up training *me.*"

Jimmy looked at the face of his grandfather who, that winter, had turned one hundred. The old man looked sixty.

"Help me untie these sheets so I can go home," the old man said. He was strapped down at the waist and shoulders.

"Nurse says you will have to stay. She says you broke your hip in two places, and your shoulder and . . ."

"You don't have to tell me my own bad luck. I know it well enough myself. Hey, Jimmy. Did I ever tell you about how Coyote the Trickster broke out of jail?"

"Many times you told me."

"Did I ever tell you why you have blue eyes and not black?"

Jimmy Blue Eyes smiled. "Because your mother had them," he said quickly, "and she was part white and part Sioux and she had eyes the color of the sky with no clouds."

"Just untie this one little sheet around my waist," the old man begged.

"I can't do it," Jimmy said sadly. "Nurse says you must stay."

The old man sighed loudly. "Jimmy Jimmy Blue Eyes," he whispered in a high whistling kind of chant. "You know," he went on whispering and whistling, "I have lived so long I can remember when men and women danced the Ghost Dance—those were great good sad times. There was a man then who wore white. He came from the desert and the people called him Numa Naha which means Our Father. This man did not drink whiskey like all others who preached."

"How old were you, Grandfather, when you first saw the man?"

"This happened when I was fourteen. And I remember how I journeyed far with my father, who was Sioux, to see this man. I remember thinking his shirt and pants were made of snow. When I got good and close, I saw that they were of ordinary cloth."

The old man looked far back into his mind as he spoke to his grandson and Jimmy Blue Eyes knew that what he said had really happened.

"I remember too how Numa Naha said that our water jar was broken and would no longer hold life-giving water from the sky."

"What did he mean?" Jimmy asked.

"He meant that the world was an old place full of new people. He said that the new people were white. He told us the breaking of the water jar meant that our lives as we had known them were done. That was a very long time ago. Yes, very long. There were not so many roads then."

Jimmy Blue Eyes stared into the dark hawk's smile of his grandfather and he knew that everything he said was true and that there had once been this white-clothed strange man who did not drink whiskey. The man had lived and gone down the one black road all must take, and now there was nothing left of him but this memory in the mind of his grandfather. Who was the man, Jimmy wondered, who?

"He was a man like any other," the old man said, reading his grandson's face. "Jimmy, give these sheets a little pull. Set me free, Jimmy," he begged.

But Jimmy Blue Eyes could not bring himself to do what his grandfather asked. He remembered the nurse. And there were his parents. They had said that his grandfather's time had come. The hospital was where he must be. The old man, they said, was bleeding from the inside; he could not live. The hospital had told them he would surely die. The voice that was talking to Jimmy was alive—that he knew. Yet it was the past that was talking. The present was not in the voice, only the distant past.

Outside the hospital windows, a red sun flamed upon the horizon. The summer hcgan where Jimmy and his grandfather tended sheep was nearly visible through the cottonwood trees. When the wind of early evening moved them, Jimmy saw the hogan and even in the hospital, which smelled of evil antiseptic, there was the stronger odor in his mind, of warm earth and piñon and juniper boughs. He could smell the good leaves of the cottonwood and the dying day's scent of the sun on all of these things.

"Untie one of these sheets and I will tell you what the white-clothed man did next," Jimmy's grandfather said.

Jimmy looked to the left and the right. No one was coming down the white hall under the bare blue glow of the long cold lights. Then his nimble hands disobeyed the orders given by his nimble mind. He untied the sheet that held his grandfather's hips in place. The sheet came away easily and fell to the floor.

The old man breathed deeply. "That is better, much better," he said.

Jimmy looked nervously down the corridor. There were spongey shoes making sounds, coming toward him, coming close.

But they passed the door and went on: squish, squish.

"Now I will tell you," the old man said. "Numa Naha told us that he had died and his spirit had taken him to the land of death from which there is no return. But something awful had happened. He returned. He woke up. He was alive once more. Then he said he was back for a reason. The Great Spirit had returned him to our world, the land of life, for a reason. And the reason was that he had something to teach us."

"What was it, Grandfather?" Jimmy asked, his eyes very excited.

"It was a dance. Numa Naha said he had a great dance to teach us. He had learned the dance from the great Spirit Father. He said that the dance was of the heart and it would protect us against all things bad. He said bullets would bounce away from the bodies of men and women who would perform his dance."

"Did you do the dance?" Jimmy asked.

Suddenly the old man looked very old and tired and in the white-lighted room his face seemed to shrink upon itself. As Jimmy stared at him, the face of his grandfather transformed from the shape of a hawk to that of a turtle, and then it was simply the old drained face of a man in a hospital bed.

"Yes," he whispered, "I danced the dance." And there was sadness in his voice, a terrible sorrow that his grandson had never heard before.

Jimmy asked, "Did the dance work?"

"No," the old man said, "the dance did not work. Many people who did it lost their lives."

"They lost their lives from doing the dance?"

"Not from the dance alone. But from the belief that the dance would save them. They thought they could dance away the wars, the bullets, the famines, the loss of lands, the deaths of their loved ones. But they could not dance back the buffalo or make the wind stir in the willows the way it once did when all the rocks were young pebbles. They thought they heard the beginning song, the one just born in the mountains. But those times were gone. There was no dancing them back. No buffalo. No protection from bullets. No great Spirit Father to save them. There was not even a dance."

And the old man's voice trailed off and was lost in memory.

"But there was a dance," Jimmy Blue Eyes said, "you said there was a dance."

"Loosen this sheet, Jimmy, and I will tell you what it was."

Without another gesture Jimmy undid the bonds that fastened his grandfather's upper body to the tilted bed; and the folded sheet fell to the floor. Thrusting his feet out straight, the old man found his freedom. Then he arched his back and pushed with his palms until he raised himself into a sitting position at the side of the bed.

Jimmy Blue Eyes did not look at him. Instead he stared out the window at the rising moon.

"Will you push that wheelchair over this way?"

"Are you going to bust out of jail like Coyote the Trickster?"

The old man did not answer. He sang a song. A nasal wisp of a song that Jimmy barely understood. The words were Navajo, old words, but only a rhythm of the song was familiar. There was a soft insistent drum in the high nasal voice of the old man and Jimmy understood the drum, and he sang along with his tongue clicking on the roof of his mouth.

The voice that was neither young nor old sang very old words in the glare of the hospital room with the newly risen moon shining in the window—

The wind begins to move
The snow starts to melt

The wind on the mountains

Makes the rocks begin to sing

The wind is coming
The wind is coming

I go
I go

In the wind, I go

When the song was finished Jimmy Blue Eyes helped his grandfather into the bright chrome chair with the plastic leather seat. Then he wheeled the old man, who was still singing the song gently under his breath, into the hallway. At that precise moment, there were no nurses in the two main corridors, and the nurse at the desk seemed to see the young boy and the old man pass before her eyes as if she were dreaming. She made no movement as they sailed silently by; she looked through them or over them, but she did not seem to see them.

Down the hall they went—the old man singing his song with new emphasis and more volume, and the boy pushing him along, humming.

At the end of a long row of quiet hospital rooms, the boy and his grandfather disappeared into an elevator. When the doors sucked slowly apart, they were on the first floor of the hospital. And people, including doctors and nurses, watched the dignified procession of chair, old man, and boy flow smoothly down the rubber mat that led to the automatic doors of the main entrance. No one said anything to them as the doors opened and closed, yet all eyes were upon them, and all ears heard the rising rhythm of the ancient chant.

Outside the hospital the air was sweet, dry, and cool, and it smelled of cottonwood and moonlight.

"Thank you for breaking me out of jail."

"Thank you for singing us home," Jimmy Blue Eyes said.

Together they sailed down the sidewalk toward the sandy wash, the dry folded hills. Together they sailed the grandfather chair made of moons, a thousand moons in the night of soft popping trees, out into the old night of newborn things.

Heron Girl

She came into the canyon slowly, her knees wobbly, her pack heavy. She knew this canyon—Little Heron—named after the sacred bird of her mother's people. The Heron of the Navajo had saved The People in their time of legends. Her father's people from Jemez Pueblo knew nothing of her feelings, or the story of Heron, or why she, a fourteen-year-old girl, would journey to a place so remote in order to meet. . .she did not know. . .

Her parents came from traditional families, but they had broken away, geographically and psychically, leaving her in the tenth grade to make up her own mind. They liked television and pizza. So did she. They seldom spoke of old ways. They wanted to get ahead, to make money, to create a new life for their children. But she remembered her mother's father on the Navajo Reservation, when she was a child, unwrapping the yellow-white bulb of a yucca root and washing his hair with it by the side of the road. She remembered how long it took to get the suds just right to soap his still-black hair.

There was this split, like a snake of lightning in the night sky.

Her mother, Navajo. Her father, Pueblo. The people of movement, of wandering, versus the people of place, of meditation. They were in her, as if trapped, these two opposite families, and wherever she went and whatever she did, one spoke to her and the other was silent. She wondered if they would ever talk together, share thoughts. Walk the harmony road.

That night, all alone by her small campfire on the sandy

beach of the Little Blue Heron River, she watched the moon rise. Her digital watch told her that it was 10:45 when the white light cleared the rocks, the great shadowy spires of the canyon. And the first thing happened: she saw, etched in stone, the reason for the canyon's and the river's name—a heron profile clearly distinguishable in the tumble of obscure rock formations. Clean and clear and looking cut by a stone chiseller's art. The long neck tucked up in flight, the feet folded, the beak long and thin, and the moon behind the whole bird, fiery and cold. After seeing it she slept soundly, even though the deep moonlight lay in pools on top of her sleeping bag.

In the early morning she heard an owl hoot—once. She arose then and dressed warmly. And without eating anything but some handfuls of trailmix, she started out on the narrow trail among the willows that led to the hotsprings.

Barefoot, she ran along the path of soft sand, making fourteen river crossings. At the fourteenth, the second thing happened: a blue heron started up from the pebble shallows, flying low and making heavy heartbeats of its great wings,so that the flight looked labored and difficult for a bird of such light-boned grace.

She stopped running, then, and watched it rise and go above the trees, higher and higher, until it resembled the bird-in-stone of the night before. Where she stood in the creek the water was warm, and she knew that in the upper ferny reaches of the stream that entered the big cold river, the hotspring waited for her. In another moment she found it, steam rising from the warm packed mud banks and rising smokily into the knife-edged hickory leaves. The water had a sour smell from the soaking nuts fallen from the trees, and the temperature was 90 degrees.

She took off her sweatshirt and went in wearing only her underpants. The waters made her skin tighten, her nipples harden. And then, after the first fear of discovery left her, she stretched out

and luxuriated in the hot primordial water. Along the banks columbines bloomed, their nodding yellow blossoms smiling upon her.

In her mind, in the water, she saw the verses of a poem. Not
the poem she had written in school which had won the Literary
Prize, but another kind. Images were jumbled like the talus stone in
the canyon; but clear to the one who could sit and make sense of
it all.

```
heron heartbeat      wingbeat
full moon        watercress, cattail
salad supper        blue-tail lizard
pumping       up and down
red-tail hawk        updraft

grandfather's black black hair
yucca pounding
suds       working deep
into scalp       gecko watching
that time of month in moon

Boy's chasing ritual,
not catching       not supposed to
daughter of Changing Woman now
a Woman now
breasts full
as the moon        cattail babies
half children       brown and
darker brown        Navajo-Pueblo
moon children        never to be more
```

She woke out of this poem-image trance, her heart pound-
ing. Was it another hiker coming? She was warned. She hastily
pulled on her sweatshirt. The third thing happened: she was crying.
She didn't know why. It was terribly sad. She was heartbroken,
crouching there in the rising steam of the hotbath—half of her

naked, in the white see-through cotton panties; half of her sweat-shirted, covered.

The sobbing continued until she felt a quick sting at mid-thigh and, looking down, saw the fourth thing: a seven-foot cream-colored snake which had bitten her. Had it been whirring on the warm bank all the time she soaked? The rattle killed the moon-babies of her dream poem. Well she knew what the bite meant. As the long snake slipped into the protective ferns, she heard its ten-rattled tail buzz one last time.

Already working, the poison warmed her chest, making her feel drunk. What should she do? She could not run for help. There was none. She could not yell. There was no one to call. She settled back into the warm sulfurous water. Heartbeat thudding in her ears; big laboring wingbeat of Heron carrying her burdens away. She stretched out in that thought, soaked sweatshirt weighing her down.

Even if she had wanted to, she could not have reached the two even-spaced bite-holes in her thigh, because they were toward the back of her, near her buttock. Unreachable. Her grandfather had once toe-herded a bunch of rattlesnakes in a hogan. He used his toe-tip to catch them up and move them, herd them along in front of him. He had been bitten, she remembered—and what did he do about it? He lay like a dog in hot mud. She remembered that was what he did. A dog whose nose sticks out of the mud, whose body is deep-set in, as if in a cast. Whose heart beats the way of the heron, slow and hard, as it climbs up into the sky.

She packed herself in, just above the spring, in among the columbines. The hot mud plastered her skin until her whole body was buried, her face looking up at the leaf-shadowed sky.

And by now the poison was everywhere in her and her heart was thudding like the heart of the great blue heron that had saved her people. She thought if she could climb on that bird's back, she would fly away to safety. The poem came to her then, and

it was the fifth thing: the fifth and final world of emergence. This was
the way all The People, both her People, had come into the world.

On bird's back   flying to my people
who are they   Ruined rock-walled place
far from grandfather helper
toe-herder of deadly snakes
my other family awaits me here
three-hundred feet above canyon

Father's family   pueblo people
rock-wall dwellers   the old ones
on bird's back   high-up cave
where they lived   nut and berry eaters
corn-growers in valley below
everywhere owl droppings in old house
the dwellers no longer here
Navajo heron leaves me
Where are the ones who lived
in the high cliffs? Find them,
find me. Lose them, kill me
They will not come.

Poison my blood, grandfather poison.
Where are the ones who make
the halves come together?
Heron gone   life lose
fern sleep   moonrise
moonset   heron's mud
snakebite   cat's head
baby bodies
cattail cry   moon hoot
owlshit.

The People have come!
I see them, offering their hands
holding their small hands out to me.

My father's Pueblo people.
Woman grinding corn.
Man with deer on back.
On the walls pictographs of snake
with ten rattles.
Alive, they are alive.

They give me their open hands!
They beckon. They say, "We are
people no more. If you see
us ever again, you will
know us only as the swallows
that live in the air of these upper walls.
You will live, Child, you will live."

Next year in the school Literary Magazine she would write:
Like a dog I slept three days without moving or eating, almost without waking.
When I opened my eyes, the sky was full of daring swallows. The old slow heron
would come out with the rising of the moon. I knew him. But now I knew the Old
Ones too. The ten-rattle poison died in the mud so that I might live, and, one day,
see and hold the babies born of halves that are now one.

MEDITATION ON
HEALINGS

The story *The Hand of Mary Tsosie* comes from Ray Brown. At the time he told it to me, we were eating fresh hot fry-bread made by Ray's wife, Ethel. Ray was saying that his aunt, a devout Baptist, used a way of divination that was a strange mixture of Navajo ceremony and Christian theology. He said her patients never objected to her particular brand of white and red medicine because her vision was strong. Medicine women, he added, were common on the reservation—not as numerous as men but just as efficacious as healers and diviners.

The Prayer Tree was inspired and mostly told by Ray's wife, Ethel, whose grandfather is a medicine man. She was patting fry-bread to be grilled on a piñon fire while she told about the bite of the centipede. The prayer feather addition to the story is of my own making. It illustrates the point that Hopi rites have found their way into Navajo ones. Prayer feathers or Pahos are traditionally Hopi. However, Navajos use them also.

Once, at a New Mexico State Track Meet where many tribes were gathered, a Navajo man appeared out of the crowd and sat beside me on the stands. I was praying for the victory of one of my favorite runners, a Navajo boy adopted by a "white-Indian" family. This Navajo boy had given me a Paho earlier in the day and asked me to "use it." The magnetism of the feather drew my visitor, who repeatedly that day expressed a desire to have a feather of his own. The national ban on eagle-killing has made it hard for many Native Americans to have feathers of the type I was holding. Repeating his name over and over, the man asked that I send him two such feathers. Then he said goodbye to me and went away. (To Alan Tom and the feathers I mailed to him, I dedicate *The Prayer Tree*.)

Heron Girl and *The Grandfather Chair* come from two similar sources, and each story features mixed-blood marriage. It is my belief that Navajos are arrogant in their ethnicity and that other tribes feel this arrogance in a way that isolates the Navajo and keeps him in his own world. Could this have come from the days of raids and plunders? The Navajos were the fiercest of warriors, as is pointed out in an earlier section of the book.

The heron story is dedicated to Loren Toledo, a half-Navajo and half-Jemez Indian. I was with him when all but the snakebite took place. In actuality, the snake incident happened to my brother. In the story I tried to convey the actual sensation of the poison as it coursed the blood, leaving the victim in a somnolent calm that also was a distinctive "high." Closer to the heart-point of the story is the relationship of the young girl and her relatives and ancestors. In the canyon she confronts the Old Ones who are more a part of her Jemez family than her Navajo one. The conflict of her life has been this split, which alienates the two families. Prior to the canyon event, the power of the female or Navajo side always has won out, but in the story, as a result of the snakebite, the two families are joined symbolically by the vision of the heron and the power of the Old Ones. In long meditations with my friend, Loren Toledo, his male presence always turned female.

Once after forty-five minutes' eye contact with him, his

man's face blurred into the image of an old woman. In the story, "he" became "she" for this reason, and because of the familial power of the Navajo family and the centering-force of Changing Woman.

One of the people who visited me when I was badly injured in a motorcycle accident in 1968 was a shy Navajo by the name of Jimmy Blue Eyes. I was told that his eyes, a rare shade of turquoise that set him apart from all other Indians I have known, were of Scotch heritage, although he also had Plains blood. Knowing the depth of The People and their way of life, I have wondered deeply about how Jimmy fared in and out of his own world.

The memory of an old man who met Wovoka* triggered this story in which the white hospital symbolizes the racial split of the boy. As in the heron story, resolution of duality comes through acceptance and wisdom and a joining with the old ways. It cannot come from the empty modern world unless it is welded to the past.

---

*The Paiute desert priest of the latter days of the Indian wars. His teachings are exactly duplicated in the story and they too symbolize the split, the divided world of old and new, Indian and white. It would be highly unlikely for a Navajo to have known or seen the Ghost Dance rituals of the Plains tribes. However, in the story, paralleling the mixed lineage of Jimmy, the grandfather follows his own father's path to meet the legendary prophet named Wovoka.

STARGAZER

In the rabbit brush up from the river, I find a familiar feather
broad plume - black moon irridescent shine - Raven.

Stargazer

Unlike most Navajos I have known, Jay is a throwback. His family fought hard against the corrosion of white society. They kept to the old ways and parented a twentieth-century shaman.

Jay's father is a holy man, a stargazer, one of the chosen ones who in the old days would look into the sky and see the future of the tribe. He could say who would live and who would die.

Jay's great-grandfather had scouted for the U.S. Cavalry in the search for Geronimo, and he had been buried at Arlington, a veteran who died at over one hundred years of age; nobody knew his birthdate and he certainly couldn't have known himself, not caring about such things.

It was through Jay that I first learned of the Skinwalkers, those wolves who walked on two legs, the werewolves of the Navajo. Jay's father had seen them looking down from the smokehole of his hogan, and he had once fallen under their spell by wearing a wolfskin he had found in a hollow tree. I heard Jay tell that Skinwalkers could move on two legs faster than any car.

"Sometime, you'll meet my father," he once told me. "Sometime soon."

Soon turned out to be sooner than I thought, and to a greater purpose than I could have wished. Jay showed up a few years ago with his father and mother. They arrived with his wife Ethel and their two children. The two elder Navajos took the first chairs. Jay's father sat far back, his grey Stetson on his knees, and stared at the ceiling. His mother crouched on the edge of her chair.

The old man spoke no English, but she spoke it well—surprising because, looking at her, you gazed back into the century before, the turquoise on her neck big as bones, the violet-tinted silk blouse loose and lovely. She wore a patterned full skirt which contrasted with Ethel's curled hair, slacks, and lipstick.

I made coffee for my visitors, and it came out strong and black; and all that was lacking of Navajo custom were the old corn-husk cigarettes, long out of style, but which, I am certain, would have been smoked with esteem that day.

Jay knew I was interested in the recent talk in the papers about cattle mutilations. After the coffee had been served, he mentioned another favorite topic of ours.

"Seen any new UFOs?" he asked.

I told him I hadn't and his father said something in a voice that had sand in it—sand on the wind, mixed with the ashes of an old campfire.

Jay and his father conversed for a while, the speech starting and stopping, a mortar of silence between each syllable, each gesture. Long silence. Talk. Silence again. Then Jay spoke to me in translation.

"My father says he saw something. Something evil. A bunch of sheep killed the other day. He says it happened at night. My sister-in-law was supposed to be watching the sheep, but she went somewhere else for a while and that's when they were killed."

"Any tracks?" I asked.

He raised the question of tracks to his father, who sat back in the chair and meditated on it. Then, after a very long silence, the sandstone voice filled the room with its wandering, wavering sound.

"My father thinks it was dogs. No tracks. Fifteen sheep killed. He says he saw two white dogs twice the size of normal dogs on that night."

Navajo stories are unravelings: they take their time getting

✧ 118 ✧

started, sometimes lead into a box canyon with no way out, then you see the tunnel with a hole of sunlight poking through: the trail to the sky.

"Were the bodies defiled?"

"What do you mean, Jay said, "by defiled?"

"Were they mauled or bloodied?"

Jay put it to his father who shook his head sadly. It was obvious this pained the old man. The story could end here, like a box canyon with no way out.

Then he spoke again, keeping his eyes on Jay, away from me. It seemed he talked for a long time in that sanded, sibilant voice of his with no pauses. At last Jay translated for him:

"My father says the sheep must not be moved until a certain passage of time. Then they will be burned. That is the only way to discourage the evil."

"Was there a lot of blood or, like some of these mutilations I've read about and seen, where there's none at all?"

"There was a lot of blood. A slaughter with nothing eaten."

"That doesn't make sense. Wild dogs, like any other predator, kill to eat, not to splash blood around."

"Maybe it wasn't dogs," Jay said.

"Then what could it have been? Your father did say it was dogs, didn't he?"

Then Jay's father entered the conversation and his mother joined in, leaning forward in her chair, far forward. And I thought that she would have been more at ease sitting on her haunches or on a flat stone before a fire. Neither the old man nor the old woman ever looked directly at me. But they were acutely aware of my presence, and what they were now saying had to do with whether I was going to learn much more, or nothing more. I could tell this, intuit it, without knowing a word of Navajo.

Jay looked back in my direction.

"My father says this thing could have been anything. Anything at all."

"Skinwalkers?"

The word came out cold, hard, I saw the old man take it in—he knew *that* word of English even if he knew no other. Now he spoke to Jay forcefully, but it was in the way I had seen Jay discipline his children, without intent of punishment, the words conveying all the intent necessary.

"My father says it wasn't what you said," answered Jay. "Says it could have been anything. Mountain lion, maybe."

Another bold move, closer or further still from my goal:

"I believe it was something else."

Jay raised his eyebrows. The old man looked impassively at the ceiling.

I continued: "I think it was evil, but I would have to know more about it."

Jay gave me a searching look—were my eyes the eyes he had trusted and which had, in return, trusted him? Was I the same man I once had been? He turned to his father and spoke again, this time there was insistence in his inflections. His father sat with his hands behind his head, then he leaned forward with his elbows on the arms of his chair and he, too, assumed a sitting-by-the-campfire position. When he sat like that, I felt he was trusting me for the first time, even though he refused to glance in my direction. He spoke to Jay and his eyes were lit up: he was saying something important.

They spoke together for what seemed like twenty minutes or more. I kept an attitude of quiet repose until they were finished. I did not want to give the impression of hanging on what was said.

"My father says to tell you that maybe it wasn't dogs. Or if it was dogs, then they were commanded to do what they did by something."

I decided to avoid using the word that offended them and

selected other words that were less volatile. "An evil intelligence?"

I saw the old man nod as I said it, though he nodded in Jay's direction, not mine, and said something else to him.

"My father says minds that can do these things are nowhere near when they are done. My father is blessed with the knowing of things that will happen in the future, and he had told me before it happened that this would happen because of something that happened before it.

"There was a Squaw Dance last summer and it was done in The Enemy Way to protect our family from harm. In the door of our house, I had found a bullet stuck in the wood. No gun had been fired at that door, but there was the bullet buried in that wood. It was an evil omen. A bad thing was stalking the house and we had to be aware.

"We killed sheep for the dance and their hides had to be destroyed, but instead, we don't know why, my father sold the hides in town. They should have been burned, but he sold them. So that evil that was in that door, from the bullet not fired by a gun, killed fifteen sheep. It was written on the skins: four lines drawn on the skins, my father said.

"Four lines for the months that would pass before the evil would strike. In November, which is now, the bad things started to happen. My father got sick and almost died in the hospital, and before that happened, when he was cleaning his rifle, he made a mistake and fired a shot at my sister and nearly killed her. But the worst didn't happen to us, it happened to our sheep, the fifteen that died because it was marked in evil on those other hides. We were lucky. The Enemy Way protected us.

"This has been going on a long time. There are those on the reservation who fear us because of what we are, the things we have achieved. But my father has wisdom and they cannot hurt him."

"So you think the sheep were slain by agents of the evil that stalked your family—dogs or something else?"

"They don't have to lift a finger to accomplish their work."

"And they never leave any tracks?"

Jay asked his father if there were ever tracks when an evil act was done, and the old man answered in swift, harsh Navajo. When he finished, Jay himself was silent a long time; then he faced his mother, who said something to him. And for a quick second she looked at me, and I saw how handsome she was, her eyes more slanted than either Jay's or his father's, her face clean agate.

"They both say they have seen tracks. Little tracks. They say the tracks are this small."

He pinched his fingers to the size of a drinking glass, about five inches high.

"Like a child's," I said, astonished.

"Like a monkey's, perfect little prints, like this."

Again, he made the size with his fingers and I felt a primordial fear of anything so small which could be said to be in possession of a malign intelligence. It made my skin crawl, those imaginary feet the size of a newborn infant. I remembered well the first time I ever heard the story of the Navajo mother who had given birth to a perfect baby—perfect, that is, except for the mouth full of developed canine-looking teeth and the hands covered with coarse hair and the feet, toenailed like an animal's, like an ape, the story went.

"And my father says he has seen the face of the thing. Not wolf-like at all. He says he has seen it looking down at him from the smoke-hole of our summer hogan. The face of an ape-thing looking down at him."

The monkey princes of Tibet, the legend of them anyway, seemed not so far as the Himalayas, and nearer to the snows of Mt. Taylor on the reservation.

Jay's parents began speaking to him of departing, but they made no movements to leave. Then, on command from the old man, each member of the family stood up. The old man said something to Jay as we went out.

Jay leaned toward me and whispered: "My father says the man who built this house is a good man."

"Tell him I am honored to have all of you in the house that I built."

For a moment Jay wondered how to translate my remark. "I think it would be easier to have my mother tell him that."

She did, and I heard him make a sound in his throat like he was clearing it. Then he got into the back seat of the two-seater pickup and kind of hunched down there, his big cowboy hat covering most of his face.

Jay's mother motioned in my direction and said one more sentence in Navajo as they prepared to drive off. Jay lingered at the door for a moment before getting into the driver's seat.

"She says you are invited to their wedding next week."

"Their wedding?"

"They were married according to Navajo custom fifty years ago to the day next Saturday. My older brother, who is a Christian, wants them to get married in a church in the Christian way."

"What does your mother say to that?"

"She doesn't care, she was raised in a mission school."

"And your father?"

"He doesn't care either. He's agreeable to it."

"Another fifty years are in the works," I said.

The old woman laughed, Jay got into the truck, nodded goodbye, and drove off down the hill with his family: six in a pickup watched over by a *stargazer* in the backseat.

MEDITATION ON
STARGAZER

In 1965 when I first met Jay de Groat, he told me his name was Joogii, which in Navajo means Bluejay.

He would tell me tales that would get only half-told—stopping when he would remember that, according to Navajo custom, they shouldn't be divulged until the spring or winter season, which usually would mean several months of waiting for me. To make up for these silences, Jay spun his own legends; one of them involved the search for a wild pinto horse that lived in the hills around his home. Summer after summer, Jay and his friends chased that horse as it moved elusively from range to range, hill to hill, always out of reach. Three months out of each year were devoted to the attempted capture of this wild creature. In a very real sense, the story of the vanishing horse, which could dance upon clouds, was a kind of heroic saga, and one which bears some resemblance to the Turquoise Horse in this book.

The gift of story-telling came so easily to Jay that I often wondered when a legend turned back upon itself and was remade in his telling. Years later, while preparing to translate the poems of "Blue-Eyed Bear," it came to me that Jay's personal legends were as authentic as the traditional tales he told of Old Man Coyote. When he spoke of Badger, drunk among the junipers on home-brewed wine, or the young mother who, glimpsing a Navajo wolf-man looking down from the smoke-hole of her hogan and feeling her life in danger, flung a wet diaper in his face, Jay was speaking from the heart of the oldest of traditions. He was shaping the words of his grandfather to fit his own time.

I lost track of Jay in 1968 and did not meet him again until 1979. In the intervening years, he had lived many lives—poet-author of *Whimpering Chant*, All-Indian Rodeo Finalist, photographer, sculptor, father. I reminded him, as we got acquainted once more, that he had once come close to saving my life. He wanted to know how. I reminded him of the accident where I was the victim of a hit-and-run driver. In the sixth month of my convalescence, and during a very low psychic ebb for me, Jay came to see me with the news that he was dying of leukemia. He said this in a very matter-of-fact way. "I should be dead in a few weeks," he said. And then he laughed it off.

At that moment, I put off any ideas I had about moving to Montana to become a poet-recluse. I married the woman who had nursed me through those crisis-ridden six months; I completed a book of poems, which the publisher insisted be printed on the handpress of Ernest Thompson Seton in Seton Village, New Mexico. (My mother told me, then, that Ernest Thompson Seton had been her mentor as a young girl. She had studied ornithology under his fine tutelage.) The marriage proved solid, the book eventually went into a second printing, the twelve fractures below the knee welded together. And, Jay, as far as I knew, was with his ancestors.

I reminded Jay, who was standing before me as I recounted these things, that he was responsible for bringing me out of a deep depression. Prior to that moment, I had been thinking only of death. Hit-and-run victimization had buried itself like a deadly pellet in my brain. Jay's laughing off his own "death" had brought me back to the land of the living.

"I did that for you?" he said, smiling.

"And whenever I needed to be reminded of it, I stared at the painting you gave me of the Blue Deer."

"Here is what I *meant* to give you," he said and put into my hands a smooth wood sculpture.

It looked like a snake twining out of the soil, but the head was the pure form of a heron.

"This is the Heron that saved the Navajo People," he said. "It is yours. Put it beside your Blue Deer."

After thanking him profusely, I brought up the remark that had haunted me for years.

"What saved you, Jay?" I asked.

"Not dying," he said, closing the conversation forever.

I
AFTERWORD

It is told, but not by The People themselves, that they came across the Bering Straits—hunters, gatherers, wanderers, herd-followers, drifting east and south. Over thousands of years the wanderers came, different ones, always on the move, always hungry, looking for something.

The ones we are talking about, Diné, spoke a language which we are told is of the Athapascan family of languages named for a lake in northern Canada. Most of these Athapascan speakers spread out and settled on the northern coasts of the continent or into the interior of Canada, becoming the Sekai people of British Columbia and the Sunis, the buffalo hunters of the Plains. Some moved on down the coast and into the region which is now California, and they became the famous basket weavers, the Hupa and Kurok.

One group, perhaps the earliest descendants of the Diné, continued traveling in a southeasterly direction, eating seeds and nuts, hunting with the sinew-backed bow, a weapon not seen in the Southwest before they arrived there; and wearing moccasins rather than sandals. These forefathers and foremothers brought with them the wind of the north and the notion of the Mother as Mastress, a permanent dislike of mothers-in-law, and a positive dread of the dead.

If such is the pre-history of the Diné, the People with the Questions (whom some of us call historians) will never know. Quite simply, the first Diné left no written report of their existence, no artifacts, and few, if any, clues of their style of life. The People with the Questions (whom some of us call anthropologists) say that the packs of Big Wanderers who came from the north were filterers and borrowers, taking baskets from California and waterproof canteens from Nevada, learning to dress in juniper bark, learning to hunt as if hunger were the only way of life.

Then the big day when—so the People with the Questions (whom some of us call archaeologists) tell us—the Big Wanderers met up with the Old Ones living in north central New Mexico, who had lived in the world of the fixed abode for more than a thousand years.

Today Diné will say the name of these Old Ones: Anasazi. But they will not say how closely or how deeply the two shadows, those of the Old Ones, those of Diné, intertwined.

And here—at this hypothetical meeting point of two worlds, one of movement and one of fixity, is where all of us become indivisible members of the People with the Questions (whom some of us call Those Who Came After). We, every one of us, do not know. Here are the usual unanswerable questions of us all—

> Did the Big Wanderers learn the art of straight-walled stone houses?
>
> Did they see the advantage of stopping and living together—sharing?
>
> Did they learn the art of an intricate family of origin-stories?
>
> Did they learn to make cotton into cloth?
>
> Did they find, for the first time, that plant of the deities, that offspring of the gods, that mystical mainstay of all the fixed peoples' existence: maize?
>
>> Corn, the only grain that cannot reseed itself.
>> Corn, the tame—not the wild seed—the Big Wanderers had known.
>> Corn, the lop-eared lovely leaf of the south.
>> Corn, the ancestor food.

Corn, the birther of the Fourth World.

Here, at this juncture in time, Diné will say: "The first People were made of corn kernels and they lived on corn." Through the corn-growing skill, the People with the Questions (whom some call You and I), tell us that the Big Wanderers, the wolves of the north, took to a new way of life and became a new kind of people: Survivors.

The year of the first-found and dated homesite of the Big Wanderers who learned to become Big Survivors is 1541. It is at this point in time that the material world of the hungry-footed wolf stayed its track long enough to encounter the deeper spiritual world of the corn-growing Old Ones, whose lives, because they stayed in one place, were more deeply rooted in the Earth. Here, the wolf paused and rested and learned the ways of unmoving meditation; the ways that go down into the ground and up into the sky; the ways that stay with the sun and the moon.

And yet the wolf would never rest, never quit pawing at the earth, never give up the wonder of the Big Wanderer. You see them today in pickup trucks, moving ever faster beyond their borders. In World War II they were Code-Talkers whose codes could not be broken. (The scalps of Japanese and German alike still hide in old forgotten trunks. Torn loose in combat, they are the bones the wolf leaves around its den; the pride-leavings of the hard-won hunt).

Now, more than ever, the restless spirit of the wolf with the rooted spiritual flower of the leaf of corn in its mouth, the way of the hunt *and* the way of the earth, is the antidote to the tired and enervated life of the people of this planet. We must, if all of us are to be Big Survivors (and not just Big Wanderers in Space), travel within and without; we must run and rest. In running, we must be willing to hunt and to fight. In resting, we must be willing to travel inward as well as upward and outward.

In the harmony of these two worlds is our own salvation,

the world at large, the continuance of the wolf with seed on its tongue, far flowering into the far distance: man of sun, woman of moon, lawless treader, root-bound believer. All these together.

II

In the Summer of 1983, I wanted to know, personally, what Big Wanderer felt in the meeting of the two worlds, the fast and the fixed. So, with the father-coach of New Mexico State running champion, Dan Maas, I went on a long trek across the Anasazi-Navajo countryside of canyon and butte and pine-barren. Together, Fred Maas, Dan Maas, and I ran the canyons. Sometimes we ran them barefoot, feeling with our own soft foot pads the hard and soft curvatures of Mother Earth. We camped under starlit-conflagrations, eating red meat over red embers. We outran a flashflood and outswam many a canyon when there was no other access. We burned our skin in biting dust and soothed it in the cool shallows of willowy Anasazi waterbeds.

In a backpack I kept my notebook. When we rested from our runs, I wrote poem-notes of what we saw and how it felt; of what Big Wanderer might have felt when the first stone-storied cliff-faces came into view; of what Big Wanderer smelled when cobs of corn smoked in the early fires of eventide; of what Big Wanderer heard when the wind combed the cliffs and caves of the corn-growers. What follows is a record of our trip, with thanks to the two men who taught me the gait of the wolf: to lean into the wind and run gentle not fast, to let the foot fall flat and to hold hands easy as paws, light at the front of the hip. These are their songs as much as mine.

1.
Anasazi Honey

Anasazi Honey-Drop
on roofbeam
stem end
    stripped cedar
    bough.

1200 A.D. yucca square—
      knot still
      visible
in lintel tie-down.

One day our cities
will rust—
    flake carbon dust

this knot will still be here.

2.
Recapture Pocket

Twang of tamarisk
in blue glade
of shade.

Anasazi axe-head
buried in dry wash.

Collarbone of a ground
squirrel by a turquoise
pebble.
 Warm wind
 owl feathers
 cows bawling
 in the sage.

Everywhere,
 evidence of the Old Ones.
All night sleeping under furry stars
 listening to the oil lamps
 leech thunder
out of sundered soil—
fill a cup   nourish a bearing
 roll a wheel
 make it possible
 to camp
 on shared/shard ground.

3.
Comb Ridge

hawk screams
jet creams
     the scar sky.

man, the molder
shaper
shunner

man, the loner
    leaper
    listener.

4.
Owachomo Bridge

The horned serpent
carved into rock

as we run
        the willow run

canyon wren toodles
        twice
scribing the mystery
        world
of change

willows whipping
        as we take
the snake loops
of this canyon

Cold-plunge the creek
        head under
blue-pocket-quiet—
        they were here,
that is all you feel.

You see eye to eye
under water:
        men of the maize
        in their
maze of stone:

men of the wolf
in their
ruff of fur.

5.
Colorado River

Dusk clouds
    send
        rain.
Yucca wands
    bend
        wind.

Reach in my bag
for toothbrush
    run the razor's edge—
        sweet cool feel
of spilt blood
        thumb's blood,
numb in the moon.

Then, an owl
    ferreting the dusk
wings by my face.
    One of its wings
is a razor of stillness:

    The wound, the radiance!

6.
White Canyon

Hum of rubber tires
on iron section
    of suspension bridge

   and,
flashflood—
      sound
        the same.

—How far to the bridge—I ask
—You can hear it—he says
    Sun-flake   snow-water
    fanning off
    lichen-beard stone.

Waiting, suspicious, for that
sudden hum of tires or torrent!

—It caught this bat—he says
    (small creature
      grim-froze)
—If sonar couldn't save it,
what chance have we?—
    (seeing in the little face
    a caught-moment
    seeing, thus, my own)

—You hear it first—he says—
like a bow being plucked,

then that death wall of water!

How beautiful, then, the canyon wren
at five hundred feet
playing the flash-flood—
like a bowstring.

7.
Bandelier

In the rabbitbrush
          up from
     the river
I find a familiar feather—
     broad plume
     black moon
iridescent shine.—Raven,
is that you, pointing the way?—
rigid featherly direction
to cave mouth.

Inside, open to the wind,
          smoke-dark
       over fire-hole:
simple shape of Raven
in petroglyph stone.—Raven,
     is that you
         shadowed in soot
         head cocked-to-shoulder
looking back down the ages
to the time when a fisherman
half a world away
loaned out loaves, and grew sick
of men.

8.
Bandelier

Two carved cougars in stone
show where the Anasazi
made their sign.
Shelters in tufa clay
round eye-hole dwellings.

I see them squatting
eating squash, grinning
    at that which
      would come to upset
their lions
and cause irreversible changes.

    —Willow baskets bend,
I hear them say,
    —so should men.

Deer and bear
crouch in summer-lofting snow,
that blinds fruit trees
by the river.

    —Men wait
I hear them say
    —they wait
for irreversible changes.

Two carved cougars in stone
show where the Anasazi
made their sign.

About the Author

Gerald Hausman began his Native American studies under the tutelage of his mother whose family had Iroquois blood. A student of the great naturalist, Ernest Thompson Seton, Dorothy Hausman taught both her sons the lore of the wood. Sid took to drawing and music, Gerald to poetry and prose. Both brothers attended Highlands University in Las Vegas, New Mexico where they came in close contact with Navajos, Ray Brown and Jay de Groat, both of whom furnished many of the ideas and stories presented in his book. In an association that has lasted over twenty years, Ray Brown and Gerald Hausman continue to swap the old ways and to furnish them with new forms.

Although both Hausman brothers are avid listeners and collectors of Native American stories, they are also teachers in their own right. Sid Hausman continues to teach songwriting workshops on the Navajo reservation and portions of this book have been presented on the reservation by Navajo children in the form of one-act plays. Gerald Hausman has taught secondary school Navajo students in private schools in the East and the West; most recently at Santa Fe Preparatory School. From 1979 to 1983 he represented various Native American artists as a fine art's representative. During the past ten years living in Tesuque, New Mexico, he has spent much time with members of various southwestern tribes.

Gerald Hausman has read his poetry aloud at such places as Harvard, Choate, the Berkshire Playhouse, the Boston Public Library, St. Johns College (Santa Fe) and the Santa Fe Public Library. Most recently the cassette of his book *Meditations with Animals* was personally presented by public high school teachers of America (through the organization S.T.O.P.) to teachers of Soviet Russia in Leningrad. Hausman is the author and editor of more than 14 books of poetry and prose.